# THE ALLERGY COOKBOOK & FOOD-BUYING GUIDE

A Practical Approach to Cooking and Buying Food for People Who Are Allergic to Foods

*Pamela Peckarsky Nonken* and
*S. Roger Hirsch*, M.D., FAAA, FACP, FACCP

GREENWICH HOUSE
Distributed by Crown Publishers, Inc.
New York

Dedicated to All Those Allergic People
Who Love to Eat Good Food

This 1984 edition is published by Greenwich House, a division of
Arlington House, Inc., distributed by Crown Publishers, Inc.,
by arrangement with Warner Books.

Manufactured in the United States of America

Library of Congress Cataloging in Publication Data

Nonken, Pamela Peckarsky.
   The allergy cookbook & food-buying guide.

   Includes indexes.
   1. Allergy—Diet therapy—Recipes.   2. Marketing (Home
economics)   I. Hirsch, S. Roger.   II. Title.   III. Title:
The allergy cookbook and food-buying guide.
RC596.N66   1984   641.5′631   84-4013
ISBN: 0-517-385724

h g f e d c b a

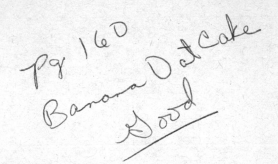

Pg 160
Banana Oat Cake
Good

# Contents

# *Preface*

Pamela Nonken loves to cook and is a compulsive collector of recipes. When her daughter was found to be allergic to yeast, Mrs. Nonken as a working mother had to find simple, appetizing foods without yeast, especially bread products, that would please the entire family, because so many commercially prepared items could not be part of her menu.

She decided to make lists of the safe products and those she would have to avoid buying. Then she compiled a group of yeast-free recipes and developed some of her own that would provide a choice of dishes. Her efforts were rewarded. Her daughter is able to eat pizza, sandwiches, French toast, and hamburgers with the family—

and she can enjoy the food without fear of allergic reaction.

Dr. Hirsch, a practicing allergist, was impressed with Mrs. Nonken's successful project and felt that her work should be expanded for the benefit of those allergic to other foods. Together, Mrs. Nonken and Dr. Hirsch designed *The Allergy Cookbook and Food-Buying Guide*. You can take it with you on shopping trips to simplify marketing, make your own additions to the products lists as you check labels, and use the recipes as a source of ideas for improvising and inventing new dishes for your household.

# Introduction

To be allergic means to react abnormally to substances that ordinarily occur in the environment. When these allergens are present in food and they produce one or more of a defined group of distressing symptoms accompanied by the presence of an abnormal substance in the blood, the individual is experiencing an allergic reaction. Once a qualified physician has identified which specific foods are responsible for the symptoms, the best treatment is to eliminate them from the diet. *The Allergy Cookbook and Food-Buying Guide* is written to help you do just that.

The task of shopping for allergen-free foods can be overwhelming because there are so many hidden ingredients. The labels listing them are often indistinct, unfamiliar, and expressed in technical language.

In the case of the common food allergens—wheat, soy, milk, yeast, corn, and eggs—eliminating the substances is especially difficult. These foods are basic in the diet. How does a person who is allergic to wheat make a sandwich? These foods often occur in a disguised form in association with other foods: Yeast is a common additive in canned soups and frozen vegetables, and soy is hidden in many foods. When symptoms persist, some apparently innocuous product may conceal the allergen and prove to be the source of trouble. Conscientious label-reading may not be enough.

The first section of this book helps you recognize the allergen; it lists each of the six common ones by its various names and in its many forms. It tells you in which prepared foods the allergen may be included, and it identifies those that are safe and those that are to be avoided. These lists do not accept or condemn particular products or manufacturers but serve instead as a general guide to alert you. Compiled between 1977 and 1981, the lists include products found locally (in our case, the Milwaukee area) and others available throughout the country. The ingredients in them are subject to change without notice by the manufacturers (depending upon the cost and availability of the constituents), *so it is still vital for you to continue to read labels carefully*. If you still have a question concerning such changes, please write to the manufacturer. The foods we describe here as "natural" have no additives.

Not only the allergy-sufferer is affected when a food must be avoided, but frequently the entire family must adjust its eating habits. Meal-planning should not become an all-consuming chore. The second portion of the book helps you prepare allergy-free food and substitutes for the favorite foods that must be avoided. Keyed to each of the general food chapters are recipes for delicious dishes with the eliminated allergens clearly designated. They are arranged by general food groups, suitable for all ages and levels of activity, and designed to avoid nutritional deficiencies, as adequate substitution for the excluded foods has been made. Enjoy them, and feel free to vary them to suit your family's needs and tastes. They're simple, uncomplicated, and just a beginning you can enlarge upon for an allergen-free, flavor-filled menu.

# Nutritional Guidelines

In our high-powered, technological society, basic nutrition varies from the "gourmet" to the "organic." A few fundamental ideas, well remembered, may help you deal with the subject.

## 1. CALORIES

The calorie is a unit of heat that describes how much energy value is in a food. If you eat more calories than you use, the excess is stored as fat. One should eat the amount necessary to maintain a proper weight at a given level of physical activity. For balanced nutrition, the calories must be correctly distributed between sugars, fats, proteins, vitamins, minerals, and fiber.

## 2. SUGARS

Sugars are a source of rapidly utilizable energy. Granulated beet or cane sugars, corn syrup, and other sweeteners may taste good, but they offer little nutritionally except calories. Most sodas, crackers, pastries, ice creams, commercial cereals, sherbets, breads, dressings, and candies have sugar added. The best way to decrease sugar consumption is simply to cook with less sugar. Fresh fruit, yogurt, and sugar-free cereal grains should be used for snacks, because they satisfy the craving for something sweet as well as provide vitamins, minerals, and fiber.

## 3. FATS

Foods high in fat content are high in calories. Diets high in certain common fats have been associated with heart and blood-vessel diseases. Most of these injurious fats may be avoided by using vegetable oils with polyunsaturated fats. Meat should be well trimmed of visible fat before cooking, and leaner cuts such as round or flank steak and lean ground beef are preferred. Milk products and cheese should contain low levels of butterfat. Fats are necessary, but only small amounts are required.

## 4. PROTEIN

Protein is essential to good health, growth, and healing. Proteins are found in meat, eggs, milk, fish, poultry, and cereal grains. Animal proteins are often high in fat, so it is advisable to use a wide variety of protein sources in planning meals. Breads, cereals, and vegetables provide some protein and have the additional advantage of providing fiber as well.

## 5. FIBER

Fiber, found in fruits, vegetables, whole grains,

legumes, nuts, and seeds, is material that the body cannot digest but needs for the normal elimination of waste. Putting fiber into the diet is easy, since most of the readily available sources are also rich in other nutrients. All of these foods supply essential minerals and are filling.

## 6. COSTS

The overall concern in planning a diet for an allergic person is nutritional value, taste, and convenience. Nevertheless, in today's economy, cost is also an important consideration. The best way to economize is to purchase basic, unprocessed foods and prepare them yourself. Convenience must be balanced against cost. Planning menus for a week in advance provides variety as well as economy. With a grocery list prepared in advance to guide you, you are less likely to make expensive, random purchases.

# *Authors' Note*

This book is intended as a guide to be used after your physician has identified the allergens responsible for your reactions. Its purpose is to help you avoid the foods which contain those allergenic substances and find the foods that are safe for you to eat.

If your difficulties persist, please consult with your physician for review of your particular case, correlation of the contributing factors, and further advice.

# Cooking Without Corn

Corn is:

Alcohol
Caramel corn
Cornflakes
Corn flour
Cornmeal
Corn oil
Cornstarch

Corn sugar
Corn syrup
Hominy grits
Maize
Parched corn
Popped corn

## COMMENTS

What is called "vegetable oil" may include corn oil without specifying it by name. However, when corn oil is mentioned it is definitely present. This same principle applies to vegetable starch and vegetable broth. Sugar or malt that is not more specifically identified may be derived from corn. It is possible for an individual who is allergic to corn not to react to unprocessed (whole-kernel) corn—for example, corn on the cob, canned corn, frozen corn, and succotash. However, processed corn (flakes, popped, parched, grits, syrup, sugar, starch, oil) may still cause difficulty in such cases. It is possible also that the meat of corn-fed chickens and cattle may produce allergic reactions in corn-reactive individuals. Even the cornstarch that is present in body powders and clothing may cause skin rashes in patients allergic to corn. The inner surface of plastic food wrapping may be treated with cornstarch to avoid sticking. Corn is often used as an excipient or diluent in pharmaceuticals, tooth-pastes, and soaps (Zest, for example). Corn may also be used as an adhesive and sealant on the inside of paper milk cartons, paper cups, and plates, and on the sticky surface of postage stamps and envelopes.

Study labels on all foods and determine if they contain corn or corn-derived ingredients. It is not possible to totally avoid corn. It is used in the preparation of more foods than any other edible material. Because of the wide distribution of corn products in food manufacture, one cannot accept the opinion of untrained personnel concerning the absence or presence of corn in a given food. A diet low in corn products can be accomplished only by cooking "from scratch."

## SUBSTITUTIONS

Corn Syrup
  molasses, sorghum, honey
Cornstarch
  potato starch
Corn Oil
    coconut, olive, peanut, sunflower, safflower oils or
    lard, butter

Cornmeal or Flour
1 cup corn flour or fine cornmeal and ¾ cup coarse cornmeal equals:
   1 cup wheat flour
               or
   ½ cup barley flour
               or
   ⅝ cup potato flour
               or
   ⅞ cup rice flour
(for additional information, see Wheat chapter)
Corn Sugar, Granulated
   Beet or date sugar (date sugar is not sugar but ground
   dates, and can be used similarly to brown sugar)

## COOKING HINTS

Safflower oil should be used for greasing of cooking
containers.

## AVOID THESE GENERAL TYPES OF FOOD IN WHICH CORN IS USUALLY FOUND

*Baby Foods*
   Commercially prepared

*Baking Mixes*
   Biscuits
   Doughnuts
   Pancake mixes
   Pie crusts

*Baking Powders*

*Batters for Frying Meat, Fish, and Fowl*

*Beverages*
   Ale
   Beer
   Bourbon
   Carbonated drinks
   Coffee substitutes made from
      grain
   Flavoring for milk drinks
   Gin
   Instant coffee
   Instant tea
   Malted drinks
   Whiskeys

**Bleached Wheat Flour**
(some brands)

**Breads and Pastries**
Cakes
Cookies
Cream puffs
Graham crackers
Pies—fruit and cream

**Candy**
Box candies, all grades
Candy bars
Chewing gum
Commercial candies

**Cereals**

**Desserts**
Cake decoration
Custards
Frosting
Gelatin
Ice cream
Ice-cream topping
Ices
Nondairy milk substitutes
Nondairy toppings
Puddings
Sherbets

**Fruits**
Canned in syrup
Frozen and pickled
Juices

**Frying Fats and Oils**
Cooking sprays
Gravies/sauces

**Jams / Jellies / Preserves**

**Leavening Agents**
Baking powders

**Margarine / Vegetable Oils**

**Meats**
Bacon
Bologna
Cold cuts
Cooked chili with gravies
Ham, cured or tenderized
Sandwich spreads
Sausages, cooked
Wieners, frankfurters

**Nuts**
Peanut butters
Roasted in vegetable oil

**Rice Mixes**
Frozen rice and vegetables with
sauces
Pre-packaged mixes with other
grains and sauces

**Salad Dressings /
Condiments**

**Seasonings**
Ketchup (catsup)

Monosodium glutamate
Pickles
Salt from cellars in restaurants
Salts
Seasoned salt
Some brands of ordinary "table"
   salt
Tabasco sauce
Vanillin (artificial vanilla)
Vinegar
Worcestershire sauce

## Soups
Creamed, thickened
Vegetable

## Soybean Milks

## Sugar
Confectioners'
Powdered

## Syrups
Commercially prepared
Dextrose
Glucose

## Tortillas

## Vegetables
Canned
Creamed
Frozen
Oriental-style
Pickled

# PRODUCTS CONTAINING CORN AND TO BE AVOIDED

Aunt Jemima Frozen Crepe
   Batter
Aunt Jemima Pancake Mix
Barg and Foster Jimmies
Beer
Beets, Harvard Style
Betty Crocker Products
   Date-Bar Mix
   Frosting Mixes
   Fudge-Brownie Mix
   Noodles Romanoff
   Noodles Stroganoff
   Pie-Crust Sticks
Birds Eye San Francisco–Style
   Frozen Vegetables

Bisquick Baking Mix
Borden's Dutch-Chocolate Milk
Calumet Baking Powder
Campbell's Soups
   Beef-Noodle Soup
   Beef Soup
   Cream of Chicken Soup
   Cream of Mushroom Soup
   Light Ones Beef Consommé
Carr's Table Water Biscuits
Cartose
Coffee-Mate
Cooking Sprays
Cool Whip
Confectioners' Sugar

Corn Chex
Corn Toasties
Country Time Lemonade Drink
Mix
Cracker Jacks
Crunchola Peanut Butter
Doritos Tortilla Chips
Durkee's O & C Real French-
Fried Onions
FFV Ocean Crisps
Flavoring for Milk Drinks
French's Worcestershire Sauce
Fritos Corn Chips
Frozen Mixed Vegetables
Geiser's Natural Potato Chips
Golden Grain Macaroni
Graf's Carbonated Beverages
Graham Crackers
Grape Juice
Green Giant Frozen Spinach
Soufflé
Heinz Tomato Ketchup
Heinz White Distilled Vinegar
Henri's Products
Salad Dressings
Salad Dressings with Yogurt
Yogannaise
Yogowhip
Hersey's Chocolate-Flavored
Syrup
Ice creams (some)
Ice-cream toppings (some)
Imperial Soft Margarine
Jams, jellies
Jell-O Pudding and Pie Fillings
Jiffy Brownie Mix
Jolly Good Soda

Jose's Tortillas, Burrito-Style
Karo Syrup
Keebler C.C. Biggs Chocolate-
Chip Cookies
Keebler Rich 'n Chips Cookies
Kellogg's Corn Flakes
Kellogg's Raisin Bran
Kix
Kohl's Chicken "O" Noodle Soup
Kosher Zion Beef Franks
Kraft Products
Mayonnaise
Miniature Marshmallows
Miracle Whip
Salad Dressings
La Choy Chow Mein Noodles
La Choy Rice Noodles
Lawry's Seasoned Salt
Libby's Vegetarian Beans, deep
brown
Lipton Instant Cup-a-Soup
Lipton Instant Tea
Malted Milk Drinks (some)
Manischewitz Lima Bean–Barley
Soup Mix
Marshmallows
Mayonnaise
Morton's Iodized Salt
Mrs. Grass Noodle Soup Mix
Mrs. Karl's Enriched Rolls
Mrs. Paul's Fried Clams
Mrs. Paul's Ocean-Perch Filets
Mullsoy
Nabisco Products
Biscos Sugar Wafers
Cheese Tid-Bits
Comet Ice-Cream Cups

Cookies (most)
Honey Maid Graham Crackers
Ritz Crackers
Nescafé Instant Coffee
Nestlé's Instant Tea
Nestlé's Semisweet Chocolate Chips
Old Time Frozen Lemonade
Old Time Fruit Cocktail
On-Cor Giblet Gravy and Sliced Turkey
Ore-Ida Country-Style Dinner Fries
Ovaltine Beverage Mix
Oven Fry Coating
Pablum Baby Cereal
Pepperidge Farm Frozen Patty Shells
Pepperidge Farm Sandwich Bread
Pet Ritz Pie-Crust Shells
Pillsbury Products
  Hungry Jack Mashed Potatoes
  No-Bakes
  Quick Bread Mixes
  Ready-to-Spread Frosting
  Refrigerated Rolls in Tubes
Piñata Corn Tortillas
Pie-O-My Pie crusts
Poly Perk Non-Dairy Creamer
Popcorn
Popsicles
Post Country Crisp Brown Sugar 'n Honey Corn Flakes
Post Raisin Bran
Post Toasties
Preserves (some)
Puretose

Quaker Cookie Mixes (most)
Rice-A-Roni
Rich's Coffee Rich
Rich's Rich Whip
Rokcach Coffee-Lite
Roundy's Sweet Pickle Relish
Royal Pudding and Pie Fillings
Ruffles Potato Chips
Salad Dressings
7-Up Soft Drink
Shake 'n Bake Coating Mixes
  Barbecue-Style
  Chicken
  Original
  Pork
Similac
Skippy Peanut Butter
Sobee
Stokely's Chinese-Style Stir-Fry Vegetables
Stokely's Japanese-Style Stir-Fry Vegetables
Stouffer's Crumb Cakes
Three Diamonds Tuna Packed in Water
Tabasco Pepper Sauce
Tuna Packed in Oil
Tuna Packed in Water (most)
Uncle Ben's Long Grain and Wild Rice
Vegetable-Oil Sprays for Nonstick Cooking
Vi-Daylin Chewable Multivitamins
Vinegar distilled from corn
Weight Watchers Frozen Dietary Dessert
Wheat and Raisin Chex

Whiskey
Wilderness Instant Apple Fruit
  Filling
Wonder Bread
Wyler's Bouillon Cubes

Beef
Chicken
Onion
Wyler's Lemonade Drink Mix

*Other products containing corn must be avoided. Read labels carefully, as ingredients may be changed without notice.*

## PRODUCTS FREE OF CORN AND SAFE TO USE

AK-MAK Crackers
Ambrosia Butterscotch Cookie
  Drops
Baker's Chocolate Bars, Cocoa
Borden's Eagle Brand Sweet-
  ened Condensed Milk
Breast "O" Chicken Tuna
  Packed in Water
Buc Wheats
Burroughs-Wellcome's "Dexin"
Campbell's Products
  Chicken and Stars Soup
  Noodles and Ground Beef
    Soup
  Pork and Beans
Carnation Evaporated Milk
Cellu Fruit Juices
Cheerios Cereal
Claussen's Kosher Pickles
Daisey Fresh Margarine

Dole Pineapple in its Own
  Juice
Fisher Dry-Roasted Peanuts
Hershey's Cocoa
Hormel canned meats
Imperial Diet Margarine
Jell-O Gelatin Desserts
Kellogg's Rice Krispies
Kellogg's Special K
Knox Unflavored Gelatin
Kohl's Peeled Tomatoes
Kraft Cheez Whiz
La Choy Bean Sprouts
Lund's Swedish Pancake Mix
Manischewitz Split Pea-Barley
  Soup Mix with Mushrooms
Manischewitz Vegetable Soup
  Mix
Molasses
Nabisco Premium Saltine

Crackers
Nabisco Triscuit Wafers
Natural Ovens of Manitowoc Sunny Millet Bread
Natural Peanut Butter (no oil added)
Nestlé's Butterscotch Morsels
Old Time Frozen Orange Juice
Old Time Margarine
ONF Co-operative Whole-Wheat Bread
PET Evaporated Milk
Postum Cereal Beverage (coffee substitute)
Pringle's Potato Chips
Puffed Rice (most brands)
Puffed Wheat (most brands)
Quaker Oatmeal Cookie Mix
Quaker Old-Fashioned Rolled

Oats
Quaker Puffed Rice
Quaker Puffed Wheat
Red Star Dry Yeast
Rice Chex
Rice Krispies
RyKrisp Natural Crackers
RyKrisp Seasoned Crackers
Snyder's of Hanover Stoned Wheat Thins, Pretzels
Sorghum Derivatives
Sunlite O J (orange juice)
Swifts Canned Meats for Babies
Vinegar from Apple Cider
Walker's "Ditex" Baking Powder
Wasa Bröd Crisp Rye Bread
Welch's Orange Juice
Wheat Chex Cereal
Wheaties Cereal

*Read labels carefully, as ingredients may be changed without notice.*

## Corn-Free Recipes

### Appetizers / Dips / Spreads

| | |
|---|---:|
| Cheese Hors d'Oeuvres | 89-90 |
| Cheese Pinwheels | 90-91 |
| Cheese Rolls | 91 |
| Eggplant Spread | 91-92 |
| Luau Chunks | 92-93 |
| Peanut Butter Crunchy Spread | 93 |
| Peanut Butter Enriched Spread | 93 |
| Ramaki | 94 |
| Tofu Spread | 94 |

### Beverages

| | |
|---|---:|
| Carob Milk | 95 |
| Citrus Sparkler | 96 |
| Counterfeit Cocktail | 96 |
| Salty Dog | 96-97 |
| Spice-Amato | 97 |

### Breads / Biscuits / Crackers / Muffins / Quick Breads / Yeast Breads

| | |
|---|---:|
| Baking Powder Biscuits #1 | 99-100 |

## Vegetables

# 2

## *Cooking Without Eggs*

Eggs are:

*Dried eggs*

*Egg albumin (ovalbumin)*

*Egg-white solids*

*Egg whites*

*Egg-yolk solids*

*Powdered eggs*

*Whole eggs*

## COMMENTS

Study the labels of all prepackaged foods and determine if they contain eggs. To prepare food, use only containers that have been thoroughly cleaned of products that have contained eggs. Avoid those foods cooked in batters, breadings, or pastries, as these often contain eggs. Check the recipes on egg-free prepackaged mixes; they may call for eggs in the final preparation. Eggs may be present in a disguised form in ice cream, custards, noodles, fruit pies, sauces, and garnishments for salads and vegetables. Egg white is frequently used as a glaze on bakery goods and candies and may not be mentioned on the label. Egg white is also used in genuine root beer to produce the foam and to clarify beverages such as wines, coffee, and consommés. Do not use foods that may have been dipped in eggs even though eggs are not part of the main ingredient.

Eggs are an excellent source of fat, protein, and iron but are not an essential part of the diet. These nutrients are readily found in other foods.

Eggs may be a source of lecithin. The product label need not list the source for lecithin included. (See the chapter "Cooking Without Soy.")

Some vaccines grown on eggs—such as those for polio, influenza, and measles—may contain a small amount of egg protein in the final product, and this may cause symptoms in individuals who are extremely sensitive to eggs. A few individuals who are allergic to eggs may also react to the ingestion of chicken and at times have nasal symptoms if they sleep on a pillow stuffed with chicken feathers.

There are no good substitutes for eggs in such foods as sponge cake and angel-food cake. Nothing else gives precisely the same aeration to the cake as stiffly beaten eggs.

Cholesterol-free "egg replacers" may or may not be free of eggs. These products are manufactured for low-cholesterol diets rather than for egg-free diets.

## SUBSTITUTIONS

Egg-free baking powder

1½ teaspoons cream of tartar plus ½ teaspoon baking soda (This mixture is to be used to replace 1 teaspoon of ordinary baking powder.)

1 egg in custard may be replaced by 1 tablespoon cornstarch or potato starch.

1 egg equals 1 tablespoon vegetable oil and 2 tablespoons water in most recipes.

Unflavored gelatin may be used to replace eggs in certain recipes.

## AVOID THESE GENERAL TYPES OF FOOD IN WHICH EGGS ARE USUALLY FOUND

### Baby Foods
Commercially prepared

### Beverages
Coffee, clarified with egg white
Malted cocoa drinks
Root beer
Wine

### Breads
Egg matzo
Glazed rolls and breads
Pretzels

### Baking Mixes
Biscuits
Breads
Cakes
Cookies
Doughnuts
Muffins
Pancakes
Pies
Popovers
Waffles

### Candy
Bonbons
Candy bars
Chocolate creams
Filled
Fondant
Glazed
Marshmallow
Nougat

### Dairy Products
Custards
Eggnog
Frozen custard
Ice cream
Sherbets

### Desserts
Bavarian
Blancmange
Cookies
Cream pies
Creams
Custards
Frostings
Macaroons
Meringues
Pastries
Puddings
Whips

### Egg Dishes
Blintzes
Coddled

Cooked
Creamed
Deviled
French toast
Fried
Hard-cooked
Omelettes
Poached
Quiches
Scrambled
Shirred
Soft-cooked
Soufflés

## Meats / Fish / Poultry
Breaded croquettes
Fricassee
Gefilte fish
Hamburger mixes
Meatballs
Meat loaf
Molds
Sausage casing
Wiener schnitzel

## Noodles / Pasta
Egg noodles
Macaroni Mixes
Pasta (some)

## Sauces / Salad Dressings / Condiments
Cooked salad dressings
Creamy Italian dressing
French dressing
Hollandaise
Mayonnaise
Newburg
Sandwich spreads
Tartar sauce
Thousand Island dressing

## Soups
Bouillons
Broths
Consommés
Mock turtle
Noodle

## Vegetables / Fruits
Fritters
Garnishes
Pies
Sauces
Scalloped
Soufflés

## PRODUCTS CONTAINING EGGS AND TO BE AVOIDED
Alphabet Noodle Soup
Aunt Jemima Frozen French Toast
Bagels Forever—Egg bagels
Betty Crocker Angel-Food Cake Mixes
Betty Crocker Stir 'n Frost Cake Mixes

Birds Eye Bavarian-Style Beans
Bouillon
Broth
Cakes (most)
Campbell's Soups
  Light One Turkey Noodle
  Noodles and Beef Broth
  Noodles and Chicken Broth
  Turkey Noodle Soup
Consommé
Cookies
Duncan Hines Deluxe II Cake
  Mixes
Duncan Hines Moist 'n Easy
  Cake Mixes
Egg-Noodle soups
Hamburger Helper for Beef
  Noodle
Hamburger Helper for Beef
  Romanoff
Hellmann's Real Mayonnaise
Hellmann's Spinblend
Henri's Products
  Sour Cream and Chive Dress-
    ing
  Yogannaise
  Yogowhip
  Yogurt Cucumber and Onion
    Dressing
  Yogurt Garlic Dressing
  Yogurt 1000 Island Dressing
Hostess Products
  Breakfast Bakeshop Donuts
    (most)
  Ding Dongs
  Ho-Ho's

Suzy-Q's (most)
Twinkies
Yellow Filled Cup Cakes
Jaeger Egg Buns
Jell-O Americana Golden Egg
  Custard
Jell-O Lemon Pudding and Pie
  Filling
Jeno's Egg Rolls
Kraft Miracle Whip
Kraft Real Mayonnaise
Kraft Tartar Sauce
Lender's Egg Bagels
Manischewitz Products
  Chicken Soup with Three
    Matzo Balls
  Egg Matzo
  Egg 'n Onion Matzo Crackers
  Gefilte Fish
  Mock Turtle Soup
  Vegetable Soup Mix with
    Mushrooms
  Whitefish and Pike
Moore's Onion Rings
Mrs. Paul's Products
  Light Batter Fish Fillets
  Light Batter Fish Sticks
  Light Batter Scallops
Mrs. Slaby's Spinach Noodles
Nabisco Products
  Chocolate Chip Cookies
  Coconut Chocolate Chip
    Cookies
  Famous Cookie Assortment
  Melt-a-Way Shortcake Cookies
  Nilla Wafers

Noodle-Roni Parmesano
Pepperidge Farm Distinctive
  Cookies (most)
Pillsbury Products
  Crescent Dinner Rolls
  Pancake Mix
  Slice 'n Bake Cookies
Quaker 100% Natural Cereal
Root Beer (some)

Stouffer's Products
  Asparagus Soufflé
  Corn Soufflé
  Spinach Soufflé
Swanson's French Toast
  with Sausage
Tuna Helper
Wish-Bone 1000 Island Dressing

*Other products must be avoided if they contain eggs. Read labels carefully, as ingredients may be changed without notice.*

## PRODUCTS FREE OF EGG AND SAFE TO USE

AK-MAK Crackers
Aunt Jemima Pancake and
  Waffle Mixes
Azteca Tortillas
Betty Crocker Rice Pudding
Betty Crocker Snack 'n Cake
  Mixes
Birds Eye Products
  Danish-Style Vegetables
  Hawaiian-Style Vegetables
  International Rice
  New England–Style Vege-
    tables
  New Orleans–Style Vege-
    tables
  San Francisco–Style Vege-
    tables
Bisquick Buttermilk Baking
  Mix

Booth French Fried Fish
  (most)
Borden's Eagle Brand Sweetened
  Condensed Milk
Brownberry Breads
Buc Wheats
Campbell's Soups
  Chunky Soups (most)
  Cream of Mushroom
  Cream of Potato
  Cream of Shrimp
  Green Pea
  Light One Turkey Vegetable
  Manhandler Scotch Broth
  Manhandler Vegetable and
    Beef Stockpot
  Old-Fashioned Vegetable
  Oyster Stew
  Tomato Bisque

Vegetarian Vegetable
Carnation Evaporated Milk
Carr's Table Water Biscuits
Cheerios Cereal
Chef Boy-Ar-Dee Products
 (most)
Chef Pierre Hi Pies (most)
Chef Pierre Pie Slices (most)
Chun King Shrimp Chow Mein
Coffee-Mate Nondairy Creamer
Comet Sugar Cones
Comet Waffle Cones
Cool Whip
Corn Chex
Devonsheer Products
 Natural Brown Rice Wafers
 Seasoned Bread Crumbs
 Whole-Wheat "All Grane"
  Wafers
Doritos Tortilla Chips
Duncan Hines Blueberry
 Muffin Mix
Duncan Hines Brownie Mix
Durkee's O & C Real French-
 Fried Onions
Franco-American Products
 (most)
Fritos Corn Chips
Geiser's Natural Potato Chips
General Mills Cereals
 (most)
Hamburger Helper for
 Hamburger Stew
 Lasagna
 Potato Stroganoff
 Spaghetti

Henri's Dressings
 Cold Blend French
 Russian
 Tas-Tee
 Yogurt Blue Cheese
 Yogurt French
Hostess Filled Cupcakes—
 chocolate
Jaeger Bread
Jell-O No-Baking Cheese-
 cake
Jell-O Pudding and Pie Fillings
 (most)
Jiffy Cake Mixes
Jolly Joan Egg Replacer
Jose's Tortillas, Burrito-Style
Kellogg's Products
 Cereals (most)
 Cornflake Crumbs
 Raisin Bran
 Special K
Kraft Cheese Whiz
Kraft Velveeta
Manischewitz Products
 American Matzo Crackers
 Matzo Farfel
 Matzo Meal
 Tam Tam Crackers
 Thin Tea Matzos
 Tomato Soup
Margarines
Mrs. Karl's Bread Crumbs
Mrs. Paul's Products
 Fish Sticks
 Fried Clams
 Fried Onion Rings

Haddock Fillets
Nabisco Products
   Cheese Nips
   Cookies (some)
   Premium Saltine Crackers
   Ritz Crackers
   Tid-Bit Crackers
   Triscuit Wafers
Nestlé's Products
   Butterscotch Morsels
   Semisweet Chocolate Chips
   Milk-Chocolate Chips
Okray's Hash Brown Potato Patties
Old Time Margarine
Ore-Ida Hash Browns
Ortega Taco Dinner
Ovaltine Drink Mixes
Oven Fry Coating
Pepperidge Farm Products
   Breads (most)
   Goldfish Crackers
   Seasoned Croutons
Pillsbury Cake Mixes
   Bundt Cake Mix
   Plus Cake Mixes (most)
   Streusel Swirl Cake Mixes
Pillsbury Products
   Butterflake Dinner Rolls
   Cinnamon Rolls
   Country Style Biscuits
   Danish
   Hungry Jack Buttermilk Biscuits and Waffle Mix
   Hungry Jack Buttermilk Pancake Mix

No Bakes
Turnover Pies
Piñata Corn Tortillas
Post Cereals (most)
Postum Cereal Beverage (coffee substitute)
Pringle's Potato Chips
Puffed Rice
Puffed Wheat
Quaker Instant Oatmeal Mixes
Quaker Oatmeal-Cookie Mix (no eggs called for in preparation)
Quaker Old-Fashioned Rolled Oats
Rice-A-Roni
   Beef Flavor
   Chicken Flavor
   Fried Rice with Almonds
   Herb and Butter
   Savory Rice Pilaf
   Spanish Rice
Rice Chex
Rice Krispies
Roundy's Pancake and Waffle Mix
Roundy's Potato Chips
Royal No-Bake Real Cheese Cake Mix
RyKrisp Natural
RyKrisp Seasoned Coating Mixes
Shake 'n Bake Seasoned Coating Mixes
Snyder's of Hanover Pretzels
Stokely's Chinese-Style Stir-Fry Vegetables

Stokely's Japanese-Style Stir-Fry Vegetables
Stoned Wheat Thins
Stouffer's Products
   Broccoli au Gratin
   Chicken à la King
   French-Bread Pizzas
   Green Bean and Mushroom Casserole
   Lasagna with Meat and Sauce
   Noodles Romanoff
   Pies
   Scalloped Potatoes
Stove-Top Stuffing Mixes
Swanson's Chunky Pies (most)
Swanson's Hungry Man Entrées (most)

Tapioca
Wheat Chex
Wheaties Cereal
Wish-Bone Dressings
   Creamy Cucumber
   Creamy Italian
   Deluxe French
   Garlic French
   Italian
   Low-Calorie Blue Cheese
   Low-Calorie French Style
   Low-Calorie Italian
   Low-Calorie Russian
   Sweet 'n Spicy French
   Sweet 'n Spicy Low-Calorie French
Wonder Bread

*Read labels carefully, as ingredients may be changed without notice.*

## Egg-Free Recipes

### Appetizers / Dips / Spreads

| | |
|---|---|
| Cheese Rolls | 91 |
| Eggplant Spread | 91-92 |
| Luau Chunks | 92-93 |
| Peanut Butter Crunchy Spread | 93 |
| Peanut Butter Enriched Spread | 93 |
| Ramaki | 94 |
| Tofu Spread | 94 |

### Beverages

| | |
|---|---|
| Carob Milk | 95 |

| | |
|---|---|
| Citrus Sparkler | 96 |
| Counterfeit Cocktail | 96 |
| Salty Dog | 96-97 |
| Spice-Amato | 97 |

### Breads / Biscuits / Crackers / Muffins / Quick Breads / Yeast Breads

| | |
|---|---|
| Baking Powder Biscuits #1 | 99-100 |
| Baking Powder Biscuits #2 | 100 |
| Banana Biscuits | 101-102 |

# 3

# *Cooking Without Milk*

**Milk is:**

Butter
Buttermilk
Cheeses
Condensed milk
Cow's milk
Curds
Custards and puddings
Evaporated milk
Frozen custard
Half-and-half
Ice cream
Lactalbumin

Lactoglobulin
1% milk
2% milk
Milk solids
Non-fat dry milk
Skim milk
Sodium caseinate
Sour cream
Sour half-and-half
Whey
Yogurt

## COMMENTS

Milk contains three major types of protein that are allergenic: casein, lactalbumin, and globulin. Of the three proteins, lactalbumin is the most common trouble causer. Casein is found in the milk from both cows and goats, but the lactalbumin in each is different. For this reason goat's milk, in some cases, may be substituted for cow's milk. It is possible that boiling the milk can change the major proteins so that they are no longer allergenic. For example, lactalbumin and globulin are denatured by heat, but casein is not. If milk is withdrawn from a diet, calcium and vitamin supplements may be necessary.

Kosher breads and margarines are milk-free. Generally, kosher baked products are free of milk. Italian bread may also be milk-free, but labels must be consulted. Nondairy products may be used in preparing prepackaged cake and pastry mixes. Some nondairy products contain casein or sodium caseinate and should be avoided.

Study labels of all foods to determine if they contain milk. Prepare foods in containers that have been thoroughly cleaned of foods that contained milk. Do not expect restaurant personnel to know what foods are made with milk or milk products.

## SUBSTITUTIONS

Goat's milk
Evaporated goat's milk
Soy-milk powder
Soy-containing milk substitutes
Meat-base milk substitutes
Nondairy creamers and toppings (whips), without casein, sodium
    caseinate, or lactalbumin
Kosher margarine

## COOKING HINTS

There are a number of fluids that might be used in place of milk; however, they do not contain the calcium, protein, or vitamins found in milk. For example, apple juice is an excellent substitute for milk with dry cereals. Various fruit juices can be used as beverages with meals instead of milk. Fruit juices can be used instead of milk when making quick breads, without altering the quality of the product. Sauces and gravies can also be made using pure broth as a substitute for milk. Fried foods can be prepared in vegetable oil rather than in butter. Safflower oil should be used for greasing of cooking containers.

## AVOID THESE GENERAL TYPES OF FOOD IN WHICH MILK IS USUALLY FOUND

### Baby Foods
Commercially prepared

### Bakery Items
Baklava
Baking mixes
Biscuits
Cheesecake
Coffee cakes
Crackers
Cream-filled pastries
Cream pies
Crumbs
Doughnuts
Pancakes
Pie crusts
Pies
Popovers
Prepackaged mixes
Rolls
Saltine crackers
Strudel
Sweet rolls
Waffles
Zwieback

### Beverages
Cocoa
Malted milk
Powdered drink mixes

### Breads
Baking-powder biscuits
Most commercial breads
Muffins
Quick breads

## Butter

## Casseroles
Lasagna
Kugel
Macaroni and cheese

## Cereals
Commercial prepackaged
  cereals (some)

## Cheeses
All cow's-milk cheeses
Fondue
Newburg sauces
Quiches
Rarebits
Soufflés
Strata

## Dairy Products:
All products made from cow's
  milk

## Dips/Appetizers/Spreads

## Egg Dishes
Omelettes
Scrambled eggs

## Fruits
Do not serve with any milk.
Some Jell-O molds contain sour
  cream, whipped cream,
  whiped topping, yogurt.

## Meats
Bologna
Lunch meats (some)
Meat loaf
Salisbury steak
Sausage
Wieners and hot dogs

## Puddings
Custard
Junket
Tapioca

## Salad Dressings

## Sauces and Gravies
Au gratin
Cream sauces
Mornay
Newburg
White sauce

## Snack Foods
Buttered popcorn
Cheese-flavored nibbles
Pretzels
Tarts

## Soups
Bouillabaisse
Canned soups (some)
Chowders

## Stuffings
Avoid using bread with milk or
  sautéed in butter.

## Sweets

Candies
Caramels
Chocolates
Cookies
Cream toppings
Frostings
Frozen novelty desserts

Fudge
Ice cream
Sherbets

## Vegetables

Au gratin dishes
Mashed potatoes
Scalloped dishes

# PRODUCTS CONTAINING MILK AND TO BE AVOIDED

AK-MAK Sesame Crackers
Alba '77 dry milk product
Alba '88 dry milk product
Aunt Jemima Frozen Crepe Batter
Baker's Milk Chocolate Chips
Baking Powder Biscuits
Betty Crocker Noodles Romanoff and Noodles Stroganoff
Bisquick Buttermilk Baking Mix
Borden's Eagle Brand Sweetened Condensed Milk
Bosco Milk Amplifier
Campbell's Products
    Clam Chowder
    Cream of Chicken Soup
    Cream of Mushroom Soup
Caramels
Carnation Evaporated Milk
Carnation Instant Cocoa Mix
Cheez-Willikers
Chips Ahoy Cookies
Chocolate Candies and Syrups

Cocoa and Chocolate Drinks, Powdered
Coffee-Mate Nondairy Creamer
Cool Whip Nondairy Whipped Topping
Cottage Cheese
Creamed soups (Celery, Chicken, Mushroom, etc.)
Cremora Nondairy Creamer
Doritos Tortilla Chips
Dreamsicles Ice-Cream Pops
Durkee's O & C Real French-Fried Onions
Eskimo Pies
Evaporated Milk
Flings (snack food)
Fudgesicles
Green Giant Frozen Spinach Soufflé
Hadley's Carob Chips
Henri's Products
    Salad Dressings with Yogurt
    Yogannaise

Yogowhip
Hershey's Real Chocolate Milk Chocolate Chips
Horlick's Malted Milk
Hostess Filled Cupcakes (chocolate and yellow)
Imperial Soft Margarine
Jell-O Pudding and Pie Fillings (some)
Keebler C.C. Biggs Chocolate-Chip Cookies
Keebler Rich 'n Chips Cookies
Kellogg's Cocoa Krispies
Kellogg's Special K
Life Cereal
Lunch Meats (some)
Malted Milks
Mazola Margarine
Mrs. Paul's Fried Clams
Mrs. Paul's Onion Rings
Murray Butter Cookies
Nabisco Products
  Biscos Sugar Wafers
  Cheese Tid-Bits
  Comet Cups for ice cream
  Cookies (most)
  Premium Saltine Crackers
Nestlé's Products
  Butterscotch Flavored Morsels
  Chocolate Chips
  Quik
Nonfat Dry Milks
Nu Maid Margarine
Old Time Margarine
On-Cor Giblet Gravy and Sliced Turkey
Ovaltine Beverage Mix

Pepperidge Farm Cakes and Cookies
PET Evaporated Milk
Pet Ritz Pie-Crust Shells
Pie Fillings—except fruit pies
Pillsbury No Bake Pie Mixes
Pop-Tarts Pastries
Post Fortified Oat Flakes
Quaker Instant Oatmeal with Dates and Raisins
Quaker Fudge-Chip Cookie Mix
Rich's Frozen Nondairy Creamer
Rich's Rich Whip
Roundy's Nondairy Creamer
Sanalac
Sara Lee Cakes
Seven Seas Caesar Dressing
Seven Seas Green Goddess Creamy Dressing
Shake 'n Bake Barbecue-Style, Chicken Coating Mix
Sherbets
Stoned Wheat Thins
Stouffer's Products
  Au Gratin Vegetables
  Crumb Cakes
  Spinach Soufflé
Swiss Miss Cocoa Mix
Swiss Miss Puddings (ready-to-eat)
Wasa Bröd Crisp Rye Bread
Whey
Whipping Cream
Whistles
Wonder Bread
Zwieback

Other products must be avoided if they contain milk. Read labels carefully, as ingredients may be changed without notice.

## PRODUCTS FREE OF MILK AND SAFE TO USE

Ambrosia Butterscotch Cookies
Drops
Baker's Products
Cocoa
Coconut
German Sweet Chocolate
Redi-Blend Chocolate Products
Semisweet Chocolate
Semisweet Chocolate Chips
Unsweetened Chocolate
Baskin-Robbin's Ices
Barbara Dee Chocolate and Peanut Butter Fun Cremes
Barg and Foster Jimmies
Birds Eye Potato Products
Bounty Products
Beef Stew
Chicken Stew
Chili Con Carne
Buc Wheats Cereal
Campbell's Products
Barbecue Beans
Bean with Bacon Soup
Beef Consommé
Black Bean Soup
Chicken Broth
Chicken Gumbo Soup
Chicken Noodle O's Soup
Chicken with Rice Soup

Chicken and Stars Soup
Chili Beef Soup
Frozen Green Pea with Ham Soup
Frozen Snapper Soup
Golden Mushroom Soup
Homestyle Beans
Manhattan Clam Chowder
Noodles and Ground Beef Soup
Old-Fashioned Beans
Pepper-Pot Soup
Pork and Beans
Turkey Noodle Soup
Vegetarian Vegetable Soup
Cap'n Crunch Cereal
Cap'n Crunch Peanut Butter
Carr's Table Water Biscuits
Cellu Rye Spice Cookies
Cellu Wheat Free Cake
Cheerios Cereal
Cocoa Puffs Cereal
Corn Chex Cereal
Cornflakes
Count Chocula Cereal
Crunchola Peanut Butter with Maple and Brown Sugar Bars
Daisy Fresh Margarine
Danish Delight Devil's Food Sandwich Creme Cookies

Diet Imperial Imitation Margarine
El Molino Allergy Cookies
FFV Ocean Crisps
Fischer Dry-Roasted Peanuts
Flavor Tree Sesame Chips and
Sticks
Franco-American Products
  Chicken-Giblet Gravy
  Spaghetti Sauce with Meat
  Spaghetti Sauce with Mush-
  rooms
Fritos Corn Chips
Frosted Flakes
Frosted Mini Wheats
Frosty O's
Fruit Loops
Geiser's Natural Potato Chips
Good Seasons Products
  Creamy French Dressing
  Garlic Dressing
  Italian Dressing
  Old-Fashioned French Dressing
  Onion Dressing
  Open Pit Barbecue Sauce
  Salad Dressing Mixes
Hellmann's Real Mayonnaise
Hellmann's Sandwich Spread
Hostess Tutti Fruit Twinkies
Imperial Diet Margarine
Jell-O Products
  Gelatin Desserts
  Lemon-Chiffon Pie Filling
  Pudding and Pie Filling (some)
Jiffy Brownie Mix
Jose's Tortillas, Burrito-Style
Kaboom Cereal
Kellogg's Products

Pep
Raisin Bran
Rice Krispies
Kohl's Chicken "O" Noodle
Soup
Kool-Aid Beverage Mix
Kosher Zion Products
  Beef Franks
  Bologna
  Salami
Krumbles Cereal
La Choy Rice Noodles
Log Cabin Syrup
Lucky Charms Cereal
Macaroni
Marv-Parv Kosher Margarine
Mazola Sweet Unsalted Margarine
Minute Rice
Minute Rice Drumstick Rice Mix
Minute Rice Rib-Roast Rice Mix
Mother's Kosher Margarine
Nabisco Products
  Comet Sugar Cones for Ice
  Cream
  Cookies (some)
  Honey Maid Graham Crackers
  Rice Honeys
  Ritz Crackers
  Wheat Honeys
Natural Ovens of Manitowoc
  Sunny Millet Bread
Nestlé's Choco Bake
Nestlé's Semisweet Chocolate
  Morsels
Ore-Ida Country-Style Dinner
  Fries
Oven-Fry Coating

Pepperidge Farm Patty Shells
Pillsbury Products
  Quick Bread Mixes
  Refrigerated Rolls
  Space Food Sticks
Piñata Corn Tortillas
Poly Perk Non-Dairy Creamer
Popsicles (most)
Post Cereals (except Fortified Oat Flakes)
Postum Instant Grain Beverage
Pringle's Potato Chips
Product 19 Cereal
Putta Puffa Rice Cereal
Puffed Rice
Puffed Wheat
Quaker Oatmeal-Cookie Mix
Quaker Old-Fashioned Rolled Oats
Rich's Coffee Rich
Rich's Rich Whip
Rokeach Coffee Lite
Roundy's Chop Suey Vegetables
Roundy's Potato Chips
RyKrisp, Natural
RyKrisp, Seasoned
Shake 'n Bake Coating Mixes (some)
Skippy Peanut Butter
Snyder's of Hanover Old-Fashioned Pretzels
Special K
Start Instant Breakfast Drink
Stokely's Chinese-Style Stir-Fry Vegetables
Stokely's Japanese-Style Stir-Fry Vegetables
Swans Down Angel-Food Cake Mix
Swans Down Self-Rising Cake Flour
Swanson Products
  Beans and Franks Frozen TV Dinner
  Beef Broth
  Boned Chicken
  Boned Turkey
  Chicken Broth
  Chunks O' Chicken
  German-Style Frozen TV Dinner
Tang Instant Breakfast Drink
Total Cereal
Twist Products
  Imitation Grapeade
  Imitation Lemonade
  Imitation Orangeade
Van Camp's New Orleans–Style Red Kidney Beans
Wheat Chex
Wheaties Cereal
Wish-Bone Low-Calorie Italian Dressing

*Read labels carefully, as ingredients may be changed without notice.*

## Milk-Free Recipes

# Cooking
# Without
# Soy

Soy is:

Soybeans

Soy flour

Soy granules

Soy grits

Soy lecithin (powdered,
liquid, and granules)

Soy milk

Soy nuts

Soy oil

Soy sauce or shoyu sauce

Miso

Tofu

## COMMENTS

Study the labels on all foods and determine if they contain soy. Soy may be powdered, granulated, concentrated, oiled, mealed, texturized, processed, cooked, sauced, finely or coarsely ground—the ways in which the world uses soybeans are almost endless.

Prepare foods in containers that have been thoroughly cleaned of any foods containing soy. Steam from foods cooked with soy, and fumes from fats used in frying, should not come in contact with soy-free foods under preparation. Do not forget that meat is sometimes fried in vegetable oils that contain soy, particularly in restaurants. Also, food served at social gatherings is seldom prepared with consideration given to the allergic person. Be careful of prefried frozen products which may have been cooked in soy oil.

Soy is a common source of lecithin, but not all lecithin is derived from soy. Lecithin is widely used by the food industry as an emulsifying agent, and its exact source is seldom listed on labels. The quantity used in foods is generally small. Most people allergic to soy will not react to such small amounts of lecithin. Manufacturers are not obligated to list the source of the lecithin used in their products; nor do they consistently use a lecithin from the same source. They can change the source of the lecithin without notice if the cost changes.

Tofu is cheese made from soybean curd. Miso is a paste made from crushed soy, rice, barley, or plums mixed with salt and water and then fermented. Natto is barley miso flavored with ginger.

## SUBSTITUTIONS

| | |
|---|---|
| Soybeans | corn oil |
|   chick peas | lard |
|   garbanzo beans | olive oil |
|   parched corn | peanut oil |
|   peanuts | safflower oil |
| Hydrogenated Soy Oil | suet (rendered beef fat) |
|   bacon drippings | sunflower oil |
|   butter | vegetable oil |

Soy Flour
   see substitutions for wheat flour in Wheat chapter
Soy Lecithin
   lecithin derived from egg yolks, plants, seeds, corn, and animals
Soy Sauce
   pure beef or chicken broth
   salt
Soy Miso
   barley miso
   plum miso
   rice miso

Soy Margarine Predominantly for Table Usage
   Pure corn-oil margarine, butter, rendered chicken fat

## COOKING HINTS

Soy flour is usually not recommended by itself for baking because of its oiliness and distinct flavor. It is often combined with other flours in commercial products. For further information see substitutions for wheat flour on page 160.

Roasted peanuts may be used as a substitute for roasted soybeans. Some individuals who are allergic to soy may also react to peanuts. In this case substitute nuts, seeds (sunflower, safflower), or parched corn.

Recipes do not generally call for soy oil in the list of ingredients. Soy oil, however, constitutes a major portion of hydrogenated "vegetable shortening" and margarines. Soy lecithin is sold in liquid form to be used in greasing cooking pans and may be replaced with sunflower or safflower oil. Olive oil is recommended as a substitute for soy oil only for the frying of meats or vegetables. Pastries made with butter, safflower oil, corn oil, or peanut oil will have the same quality and taste as those made with soy oil. Ground meat "extenders" contain soy because of the high protein content of the soy. The addition of 1 egg per 1 pound of ground meat plus ½ cup crisp, ready-to-eat cereal will "extend" the meat in the same way.

## AVOID THESE GENERAL TYPES OF FOOD IN WHICH SOY IS USUALLY FOUND

### Baby Foods
Commercially prepared

### Bakery Goods and Mixes
Breadings
Breads
Cakes
Coffee cake
Cookies
Crackers
Doughnuts
Pancakes
Pies
Rolls
Stuffings
Sweet rolls
Waffles

### Beverages
Coffee substitutes
Drink mixes

### Candies
Caramels
Chocolate candy
Gelatin candy
Hard candy
Nut candy

### Cereals
Processed breakfast cereals

### Condiments
Flavor enhancers
Synthetic spices and seasonings

### Dairy Products
Cheese (some)
Dips
Milk substitutes
Nondairy creamer
Nondairy whipped topping
Tofu

### Desserts
Dumplings
Ice cream
Ice-cream cones
Pastries
Puddings

### Meats
Frozen meat patties
Frozen fish patties
Hamburger extenders
Lunch meats
Sausage

*Pasta*
Macaroni
Noodles
Spaghetti

*Salad Dressings and*
*Mayonnaise*

*Sandwich Spreads*

*Shortening / Oil /*
*Margarine*

*Snack Foods*
Corn chips
Potato chips
Soy nuts

*Soups*

*Vegetables*
Soy sprouts
Canned and frozen oriental-
style vegetables
Canned and frozen vegetables
in sauces

## PRODUCTS CONTAINING SOY AND TO BE AVOIDED

Angelo's Italian-Style Bread
Archway Cookies
Aunt Jemima Frozen Crepe
Batter
Aunt Jemima Frozen Pancake
Batter
Austin's Cheez on Cheez Sand-
wiches
Azteca Tortillas
Bacos (imitation bacon chips)
Baker's Semisweet Chocolate
Baker's Semisweet Chocolate
Morsels
Barg and Foster Candies
Barg and Foster Tangy Twisters
Betty Crocker Products
Cake mixes (most)
Noodle mixes (most)
Potato mixes (most)
Snackin' Cake mixes

Bisquick Baking Mix
Bit-O-Honey Candy Bars
Blue Bonnet Margarine
Borden's Dutch Chocolate Chip
Ice Cream
Borden's Real Butter Pecan Ice
Cream
Breads, packaged (most)
Brownberry Breads
Burry Crackers
Campbell's Soups
Cream of Celery
Cream of Mushroom
Noodle and Chicken Broth
Old-Fashioned Tomato and
Rice
Tomato
Vegetable
Vegetable with Beef Stock
Vegetarian Vegetable

Carnation Instant Breakfast
Carr's Table Water Biscuits
Cellu Products
 French Dressing
 Soyannaise
 Soy Flakes
Cheetos Corn Snacks
Chef Boy-Ar-Dee Cannelloni
Chef Pierre Frozen Hi-Pie
Chiffon Margarine
Coffee-Mate Nondairy Creamer
Cookies, packaged (most)
Corn curls (any kind)
Cracker Jacks
Crisco Oil
Crosse and Blackwell's Salad
 Dressing
Crunchola Peanut Butter with
 Maple and Brown Sugar
Daisy Fresh Margarine
Dare Cookies
Dean's Products
 Bacon Horseradish Dip
 Bermuda Onion Dip
 Garlic Dip
Derby Steak Sauce
Devonshire Melba Toast
Devonshire Plain Bread Crumbs
Diet Imperial Imitation Margarine
Doritos Tortilla Chips
Duncan Hines Baking Mixes
Durkee's O & C French Fried
 Onions
Eggo Frozen Waffles
EPK French Dressing
Ev-R-Crisp Sugar Cones
FFV Cookies

Fiddle Faddle Snacks
Franco-American Products
 RavioliOs
 Rotini and Meatballs
 SpaghettiOs with Meatballs
French's Worcestershire Sauce
Fritos Corn Chips
General Foods International
 Coffees
Golden Delight Frozen Waffles
Golden Grain Rice-A-Roni Mixes
Hamburger Helper Dinner Mixes
Heinz Worcestershire Sauce
Hellmann's Real Mayonnaise
Henri's Products
 Salad Dressing (most)
 Yogannaise
 Yogowhip
Hershey's Candies
Hershey's Chocolate Syrup
Hillbilly Old-Fashioned Bread
Hoffman House Tartar Sauce
Honeycomb Cereal
Hormel Chili Without Beans
Hostess Products
 Crumbcakes
 Cupcakes
 Ho-Ho's
 Twinkies
Hunt's Snack Pack Puddings
Imperial Margarine (soft)
Jaeger Bread
Jif Peanut Butter
Jell-O Instant Pudding and Pie
 Fillings
Jiffy Brownie and Cake Mixes
Jiffy Frosting Mixes

Johnston's Graham Cracker Ready Crust
Johnston's Hot Fudge
K-Biscuits
Keebler Cookies (most)
Kellogg's Raisin Bran
Kraft Products
  Egg Noodles and Chicken
  Miracle Whip
  Salad Dressings
  Real Mayonnaise
  Tartar Sauce
La Choy Products
  Chow Mein Noodles
  Rice Noodles
  Soy Sauce
Lea & Perrins Worcestershire Sauce
Life Cereal
Lov-It-Butterup Table Spread
M & M Candies
Mama's Ring Cookies
Marathon Bar
Marv-Parv Margarine
Maull's Steak Sauce
Maurice Lenell Cookies
Mazola No-Stick Spray
Mazola Sweet Unsalted Margarine
Mrs. Grass Noodle Soup Mix
Mrs. Karl's Breads
Murray's Cookies
Nabisco Products
  Cinnamon Treats
  Comet Cups (ice-cream cones)
  Cookies (most)
  Crackers
  Graham Crackers

Graham-Cracker Crumbs
Honey Maid Graham Crackers
Premium Saltine Crackers
Ritz Crackers
Triscuits
Zwieback Toast
Natural Ovens of Manitowoc
  Sunny Millet Bread
Nature Valley Granola Products
Nestlé's Products
  Butterscotch Morsels
  Choco Bake
  Cookie Mixes
  Quik (Beverage Mix)
  Semisweet Chocolate Chips
Nuspread Vegetable Oil Spread
Old Time Margarine
Old Time Salad Dressing
On-Cor Giblet Gravy and Sliced Turkey
Ore-Ida Country-Style Dinner Fries
Ovaltine Beverage Mix (malt flavor)
Oven Fry Coating for Chicken
Pam Cooking Spray
Parkay Margarine
Pepperidge Farm Products
  Breads
  Cookies
  Frozen Pastries
Pet Ritz Pie Crust
Pillsbury Products
  Cherry Nut Quick Breads
  Figurines
  Flakey Turnover Pies
  Ready-to-Spread Frosting

Refrigerated Rolls
Poly Perk Non-Dairy Creamer
Pringle's Potato Chips
Promise Margarine
Puritan Oil
Quaker Cookie Mixes
Quaker Instant Oatmeal with
    Bran and Raisins
    Raisins and Spice
Reese's Peanut Butter Cups
Reezon Seasoning
Richelieu Salad Dressings
Rich's Coffee Rich
Roman Meal Frozen Waffles
Roundy's Frozen Waffles
Roundy's Instant Nondairy
    Creamer
Ruffles Potato Chips
Salerno Cookies
Salerno Crackers
Sara Lee Frozen Pastries
Seven Seas Salad Dressings
Sexton Sauces
    Chop Suey Sauce

Mushroom Sauce
Sirloin Sauce
Shake 'n Bake Coating Mixes
    (most)
Skippy Peanut Butter
Smucker's Toppings (some)
Starburst Fruit Chews
Stark Candy Raisins
Stokely's Chinese-Style Stir-Fry
    Vegetables
Stokely's Japanese-Style Stir-
    Fry Vegetables
Stoned Wheat Thins
Stouffer's Spinach Soufflé
    Side Dish
Stove-Top Stuffing
Taco Shells (most)
Wesson Oil
Wheat Chex with Raisins
Wish-Bone Salad Dressings
Wonder Bread
Worcestershire Sauces
Wyler's Lemonade Mix
Zevo Cultured Food Dressing

*Other products containing soy must be avoided. Read labels carefully, as ingredients may be changed without notice.*

## PRODUCTS FREE OF SOY AND SAFE TO USE

AK-MAK Sesame Crackers
Bagels Forever (plain and egg)
Baker's German Sweet Choco-
    late

Barg & Foster Red Laces
Bay's English Muffins
Betty Crocker Hash Browns
    with Onion

Betty Crocker Potato Buds
Borden's Products
  Dutch Chocolate Natural-
    Flavor Ice Cream
  Eagle Brand Sweetened
    Condensed Milk
  Lime Sherbet
  Maple Nut Ice Cream
  Rainbow Sherbet
Brach's Products
  Lozenges
  Root Beer Barrels
  Spicettes
  Starlight Mints
Buc Wheats Cereal
Butter
Campbell's Products
  Beef with Vegetables and
    Barley Soup
  Chicken Gumbo Soup
  Chicken Noodle Soup
  Cream of Chicken Soup
  Noodles and Beef Broth
  Turkey Vegetable Soup
  Vegetable Beef Consommé
  Vegetable Beef Soup
Carnation Evaporated Milk
Cheerios Cereal
Cheeses (most)
Chef Boy-Ar-Dee (most products)
Coco Wheats Cereal
Cool Whip
Corn Chex Cereal
Creamettes Macaroni and
  Cheese Dinner
Cream of Wheat Cereal
Cremora Nondairy Creamer

Dean's French Onion Dip
Egg Beaters Egg Substitute
Famous Chocolate Wafers
Fischer Dry-Roasted Peanuts
Flavor-Kist Soda Crackers
Fleischmann's Margarines
Franco-American SpaghettiOs
French's Big Tate
French's Mustard
Geiser's Potato Chips
General Mills Golden Grahams
  Cereal
Heinz Tomato Ketchup
Henri's Russian Dressing
Henri's Tastee Dressing
Hills Bros. Instant Coffee
  Beverages
Hormel Chili with Beans
Hungry Jack Mashed Potatoes
Jaeger Egg Buns
Jell-O Gelatin Desserts
Jolly Joan Egg Replacer
Jolly Joan Rice Bran
Jose's Tortillas Burrito-Style
Keebler's Vanilla Wafers
Kellogg's Products
  Cornflake Crumbs
  Frosted Flakes
  Mini Wheats
  Rice Krispies
  Special K
Kosher Zion Beef Franks
Kraft Products
  American-Style Spaghetti
    Dinner
  Marshmallow Creme
  Party Mints

Tangy Italian-Style Spaghetti Dinner
Lawry's Seasoned Salt
Manischewitz Products
  Dark Chocolate Crunch Bar
  Matzo Farfel
  Matzo Meal
  Thin Tea Matzos
  Vegetable Soup Mix with Mushrooms
Mazola Corn Oil
Milk Mate Flavored Syrup
Mrs. Karl's White-Lite Bread
Nabisco Products
  Cream of Wheat
  Cracker Meal
  Shredded Wheat
Old Time Old Fashioned Peanut Butter
Ore-Ida Hash Browns
Oscar Mayer Beef Franks
Ovaltine Beverage Mix (chocolate flavor)
PET Evaporated Milk
Pillsbury Farina
Piñata Corn Tortillas
Planters Peanut Oil
Poly-Soft Safflower Oil
Post Raisin Bran
Postum
Puffed Rice

Puffed Wheat
Quaker Products
  Instant Oatmeal with Apples and Cinnamon
  Instant Oatmeal with Maple and Brown Sugar
  Oatmeal (Regular flavor)
  Old-Fashioned Rolled Oats
  100% Natural Cereals
Rice Chex
Rich's Rich Whip
Roundy's Products
  Chop Suey Vegetables
  Potato Chips
  Salad Mustard
RyKrisp (natural and seasoned)
Smucker's Toppings
  Caramel
  Pineapple
  Strawberry
Snyder's of Hanover Pretzels
So-Kreem Chives Dip
Sunlight Oil
Swift's Beef Franks
Swiss Knight Fondue
Swiss Miss Hot-Cocoa Mix
Van Camp's New Orleans–Style Red Kidney Beans
Wheat Chex
Wheaties
Wyler's Bouillon Cubes

*Read labels carefully, as ingredients may be changed without notice.*

## Soy-Free Recipes

# 5

# *Cooking*
# *Without*
# *Wheat*

Wheat is:

| | |
|---|---|
| Bran | Wheat flour |
| Buckwheat | Wheat germ |
| Buckwheat groats | Wheat gluten |
| Farina | Wheat starch |
| Graham flour | White enriched flour |
| Malt | Whole-wheat flour |

MSG (monosodium glutamate; not all MSG comes from wheat, but wheat is a common source)

## COMMENTS

Study the labels on all foods and determine if they contain wheat. Prepare foods in containers that have been thoroughly cleaned of stuffings, dressings, sauces, and gravies made with wheat or wheat flour. Steam from foods cooked with wheat, and fumes from fats used in frying foods with wheat, should not come in contact with the wheat-free foods under preparation. Do not overlook as a source of allergen meat fried in fat that has been previously used to fry meats rolled in flour, particularly in restaurants and in other people's homes. Do not expect restaurant personnel to be accurate when describing food preparation.

Malt and malted cereal syrup may be derived from wheat, but are usually derived from barley.

## SUBSTITUTIONS

1 cup wheat flour equals:
½ cup barley flour

or
¾ cup coarse cornmeal
or
⅝ cup potato flour
or
⅞ cup rice flour
or
1 ¼ cup rye flour
or
1 cup rye meal
or

1 1/3 cup rolled oats (ground)
or
2/3 cup oat flour
or
½ cup rye flour plus
½ cup potato flour
or
2/3 cup rye flour plus
1/3 cup potato flour
or
⅝ cup rice flour plus
1/3 cup potato flour

1 tablespoon wheat flour equals:
½ tablespoon cornstarch
or
½ tablespoon potato-starch flour
or
½ tablespoon rice starch
or
½ tablespoon arrowroot starch

## COOKING HINTS

Coarser meals and flours require more leavening. Use 2½ tablespoons baking powder per cup of coarse flour. Sift 5 or 6 times. Bake longer at lower temperatures.

Cake made from flours other than wheat may be dry. Fruits, chocolate chips, and nuts added to cakes will improve textures.

Cornmeal products have a grainy texture. If cornmeal is cooked or scalded after measuring, a smoother texture will result.

Potato flour (or potato starch) is best used in sponge cakes. It also makes an excellent breading for meat, fish, and poultry.

Soy flour is usually not recommended for baking by itself because of its oiliness and distinct flavor. However, it is satisfactory when combined with potato flour.

GROUND OAT FLOUR and whole-grain oats can be used to thicken soups, gravies, sauces, stews, and puddings. GROUND OAT FLOUR can be substituted directly for all-purpose flour when thickening.

Because it is a whole-grain, GROUND OAT FLOUR is not as highly refined as all-purpose flour. White sauces will tend to have a creamier color and not as smooth a texture. Gravies, cheese sauces, soups, and stews will not look or taste very different but will be more nutritious. TOASTED OATS can be used in place of bread crumbs, unprocessed bran, or wheat germ, and in some cases you can substitute TOASTED OATS for nuts.

## GROUND OAT FLOUR

1. Place 1 to 1½ cups uncooked rolled oats in blender or food processor.
2. Blend or process for about 60 seconds.
3. Store in tightly covered container in cool, dry place up to 6 months. Use for baking, thickening, or dredging and browning.

## TOASTED OATS

1. Place 1 to 2 cups uncooked rolled oats in ungreased 15½ x 10½-inch jelly-roll pan or an equivalent-size cookie sheet.
2. Bake in preheated, moderate oven, 350°, 15 to 20 minutes or until light golden brown.
3. Cool; store in tightly covered container in refrigerator up to 6 months.

*Makes 1 to 2 cups TOASTED OATS.*

For 2 to 3 cups TOASTED OATS, increase baking time to 20 to 25 minutes.

To toast oats in quantity, divide contents of one 18-ounce tube between two ungreased 15½ x 10½-inch jelly-roll pans; increase baking time to 25 to 30 minutes.

## AVOID THESE GENERAL TYPES OF FOOD IN WHICH WHEAT IS USUALLY FOUND

*Baby Foods*
  Commercially prepared

*Bakery Goods*
  Biscuits
  Bran muffins
  Coffee cake
  Corn bread
  Crackers
  Croutons
  Doughnuts
  Gluten bread
  Graham bread
  Matzo

  Matzo cake meal
  Matzo farfel
  Matzo meal
  Muffins
  Pancakes
  Popovers
  Pretzels
  Rolls
  Rusks
  Rye bread
  Soy bread
  Sweet rolls
  Waffles
  White bread

Whole-wheat bread
Zwieback

### Beverages
Ale
Beer
Coffee substitutes
Gin
Prepared milk drinks made
with cereal additives or malt
Whiskey or any drink containing neutral spirits

### Breaded Foods
Bread crumbs
Breading mixtures
Cracker crumbs

### Cereals
Wheat cereals and those containing wheat or wheat products including bran

### Cheeses
Processed cheese and flavored cottage cheese products containing wheat stabilizers

### Desserts
Cakes
Cookies
Custards
Dumplings
Ice-cream cones
Pastries
Pies

Puddings

### Fruits
Any fruit prepared or served with a sauce thickened with any wheat flour or coming in contact with any wheat product

### Meats/Poultry/Fish
Bologna (some)
Bread and cracker stuffings
Canned meats (unless guaranteed pure meat)
Chili con carne
Croquettes
Fish patties
Hamburger fillers and extenders
Knockwurst (some)
Liverwurst (some)
Lunch meats (some)
Meat loaf
Meat patties
Salami (some)
Sausages (some)
Swiss steak
Wieners and hot dogs (some)

### Pasta
Alphabet noodles
Dumplings
Linguine
Macaroni
Matzo farfel
Mustaccioli

Noodles
Ravioli
Soup rings
Spaghetti
Vermicelli

## Prepared Mixes
Biscuit
Bran muffins
Bread mix
Cake
Cookie
Corn bread
Corn muffins
Doughnut
Ice Cream
Muffin
Pancake
Pie crust
Potato mix
Pudding
Quick bread
Rice mix
Roll mix
Rye bread
Rye rolls
Soybean mix
Waffle

## Salad Dressings / Condiments

## Sauces and Gravies
Butter sauce
Gravy
Cream sauce
White sauce

## Snack Foods

## Soups
Bisques
Chowders
Cream soups
Meat soups
Vegetable soups

## Sweets
Chocolates
Commercial candies

## Vegetables
Any vegetable prepared or served with a sauce thickened with wheat flour or coming in contact with any wheat product

# PRODUCTS CONTAINING WHEAT AND TO BE AVOIDED

AK-MAK Crackers
Bachman Products
  Pretzel B's

Pretzel Logs
Pretzel Sticks
Betty Crocker pastry mixes

Buc Wheats Cereal

Campbell's Soups, canned and frozen, especially those with noodles

Cap'n Crunch Cereal

Carnation Chocolate-Malt Ice Cream

Carr's Table Water Biscuits

Cheerios Cereal

Cheez Willikers

Chef Pierre Frozen Pies

Cocoa Puffs Cereal

Cocomalt Beverage Mix

Count Chocula Cereal

Cracklin' Bran Cereal

Cream of Wheat Cereal

Crunchola Peanut Butter with Maple and Brown Sugar Bars

Doritos Tortilla Chips

Durkee's O & C Real French-Fried Onions

Eckrich's products
  Chipped Sliced Chicken
  Chipped Smoked Turkey
  Imitation Chicken

Farina

Frosty O's

Grape Nuts

Heinz Soups, canned and frozen, especially those with noodles

Heinz White Distilled Vinegar

Herb Ox Bouillon Cubes

Hershey's Fortified Chocolate Syrup

Honey Wheats

Jay's Onion and Garlic Chips

Jiffy Mixes

Jose's Tortillas Burrito-Style

Kaboom Cereal

Keebler Cookies

Kellogg's Products
  All Bran
  Apple Jacks
  Bran Buds
  Bran Flakes
  Cocoa Krispies
  Frosted Flakes
  Frosted Mini-Wheats
  Fruit Loops
  Krumbles
  Pep
  Product 19
  Raisin Bran
  Special K
  Sugar Smacks

Kikkoman Soy Sauce

Kohl's Soups, canned and frozen, especially those with noodles

Kroger's Country Club Salami and Bologna

La Choy Rice Noodles

La Choy Chow Mein Noodles

Lawry's Spaghetti Mix

Life Cereal

Lucky Charms Cereal

Malted Milk Balls

Malt-O-Meal

Manischewitz Party Mixes

Manischewitz Soup Mixes

Marukan Rice Vinegar

Mrs. Paul's Frozen Food Products

Muffets Cereal

Nabisco Products
  Biscos Sugar Wafers

Cheese Tid-Bits Crackers
Cookies (most)
Honey Maid Grahams
Premium Saltines
Ritz Crackers
Triscuits
Ovaltine Drink Mixes
Oven Fry Coating
Pepperidge Farm Pastries and Cookies
Pet Ritz Pie Shells
Petti John's Pastries
Pillsbury Ready-to-Spread Frosting
Pop-R-Corns
Post Country Crisps Brown Sugar 'n Honey Cornflakes
Post Raisin Bran
Postum Instant Grain Beverage
Puffed Wheat
Quaker Products
  Instant Oatmeal with Bran and Raisins
  Instant Oatmeal with Raisins and Dates
Oatmeal Cookie Mixes
Ring-O-Lings Snack Food
Sara Lee Coffee Cakes and Pastries
Shake 'n Bake Coating Mixes (most)
Shredded Wheat
Snyder's of Hanover Pretzels
Stoned Wheat Thins
Stouffer's Pastries
Swift's Premium Brown 'n Serve Sausages
Team Cereal
Total Cereal
Wheat Chex
Wheat Chex and Raisins
Wheat Chips
Wheatena Cereal
Wheaties Cereal
Wheat Thins
Whistles Snacks
Wonder Bread
Wyler's Bouillon Cubes

*Other products containing wheat must be avoided. Read labels carefully, as ingredients may be changed without notice.*

## PRODUCTS FREE OF WHEAT AND SAFE TO USE

Alpha Bits Cereal
Armour Boneless Ham
Armour Vienna Sausage
Azteca Corn Tortillas
Baker's Baking Chocolate Chips

Baker's Cocoa
Barg & Foster Jimmies
Borden's Cottage Cheese
  (unflavored)
Borden's Eagle Brand Sweetened
  Condensed Milk
Bounty Corn Beef Hash
Bugle Snacks
Campbell's Products
  Beans and Franks
  Home-Style Beans
  Old-Fashioned Beans
  Pork and Beans
  Tomato Juice
  V-8 Cocktail Juice
Campbell's Soups
  Bean Broth
  Bean with Bacon
  Beef Broth
  Black Bean
  Chicken Gumbo
  Chicken with Rice
  Consommé
  Frozen Fish Chowder
  Green Pea
  Frozen Green Pea with Ham
  Frozen Old-Fashioned Vege-
    table with Beef
  Frozen Oyster Stew
  Vegetable Bean
Calumet Baking Powder
Caramel Corn
Carnation Evaporated Milk
Cellu Products
  Cereal-Free Baking Powder
  Corn Flour

Oatmeal Cookies
Rice Cookies, Flour, Wafers
Rye Cookies
Soyannaise
Soybean Flour, Wafers
Certo Fruit Pectin
Cheese-Flavored Popcorn
Cheeses (natural)
China Bowl Cellophane Noodle
  and Rice Sticks
Chipos Snacks
Clabber Girl Baking Powder
Coffee-Mate
Cool Whip
Corn Chex
Corn Chips
Cream of Rice
Demet's Turtles (candy)
Dream Whip Topping
El Molino Allergy Cookies
Franco-American Spaghetti Sauce
  with Mushrooms
French's Prepared Mustard
Fritos Corn Chips
Frozen French-fried potatoes
Fruits, fresh and frozen without
  syrup
Geiser's Natural Potato Chips
Golden Griddle Pancake Syrup
Good Seasons Salad-Dressing
  Mixes
Heath Bars Candy
Heinz Catsup
Hellmann's Real Mayonnaise
Hershey's Candy Bars and Choco-
  late Squares

Hershey's Cocoa
Hollywood Butter Nut Candy Bar
Holsum Old-Fashioned Peanut Butter
Honey Comb cereal
Hormel Brown 'n Serve sausage
Hormel Spam
Ice cream (read labels carefully)
Jell-O Gelatin Desserts
Jell-O Pudding and Pie Fillings
Jolly Joan Rice Bran
Karo Syrups
Kellogg's Products
  Cornflakes
  Rice Krispies
  Sugar Pops
Kool-Aid Drink Mixes
Kosher Zion Franks
Korkers Snacks
Kraft Products
  American Cheese
  Caramels
  French Dressing
  Marshmallows
  Miracle Whip
  Philadelphia Cream Cheese
  Roquefort Dressing
Libby's Tropi-Cal Fruit Punch
Life Savers Candy
Log Cabin Syrup
M & M Candies (plain and peanut)
Mars Candy Bars
Maxwell House Instant Coffee
Nestlé's Products
  Butterscotch Morsels
  Chocolate Candy Bars

Quik Beverage Mix
Nescafé Instant Coffee
Semisweet Chocolate Chips
Oatmeal and Rolled Oats
Old Manse Syrups
Old Time Margarine
Ore-Ida Hash Browns
Oscar Mayer Beef and Regular Franks
Pearsons Mint Patties
PET Evaporated Milk
Piñata Corn Tortillas
Pringle's Potato Chips
Puffa Puffa Rice
Puffed Rice
Quaker Instant Oatmeal
  Apples and Cinnamon
  Maple and Brown
  Plain
Quaker Old Fashioned Rolled Oats
Rice cakes
Rice Chex Cereal
Rice Flakes Cereal
Rice Honeys Cereal
Rice Krinkles Cereal
Roundy's Potato Chips
RyKrisp (natural and seasoned)
Sinai-48 Kosher Franks
Skippy Peanut Butter
Stokely's Chinese-Style Stir-Fry Vegetables
Stokely's Japanese-Style Stir-Fry Vegetables
Swanson's Products
  Beef Broth
  Boned Chicken

Boned Turkey
Chicken Broth and Spread
Chunks 'O Chicken
Swift's Beef and Regular Franks

Three Musketeers Candy Bars
Tootsie Rolls Candy
Vegetable Oils

*Read labels carefully, as ingredients may be changed without notice.*

## Wheat-Free Recipes

### Appetizers / Dips / Spreads

# Cooking
# Without
# Yeast

Yeast Is:

Baker's yeast (used as a leavening
    agent)
Brewer's yeast (used as a ferment-
    ing agent)
Compressed yeast (active)
Dry yeast
"Natural" vitamins derived from
    yeast

## COMMENTS

It is impossible to avoid yeast completely. Yeast spores
occur naturally in the air and grow rapidly on any source
of carbohydrate and water. Consequently the recipes
mentioned in this section and throughout the rest of this

book may not be totally yeast-free. The effect of extremely small amounts of yeast allergens dissolved in foods when the occasional yeast particle is present, whether actively growing or not, has never been reliably measured. Therefore the degree of sensitivity of the patient allergic to yeast is the most important factor in determining whether symptoms will occur upon contact with yeast. That is, the more allergic the patient, the more likely it is that he or she will react to the allergen. Only a physician can judge the degree of sensitivity with sufficient accuracy to advise patients whether or not they will react to a tiny amount of yeast allergen.

Patients who are allergic to molds may also react to yeasts, since both are fungi and may share common allergens. It sometimes happens that a patient allergic to yeast may "crossreact" and develop symptoms from ingestion or inhalation of a mold. For example, mushrooms, which are a fungus just as molds and yeasts are fungi, may share common allergens and may cause reactions as a yeast does in patients allergic to yeast. It might be assumed that fresh mushrooms would grow yeast; however, recent laboratory experiments have shown that when efforts were made to culture yeast from fresh mushrooms, only mold could be grown rather than yeast. Since patients allergic to yeast may also crossreact to mold, we do not advise such patients to eat mushrooms, although not all patients exhibit crossreactivity.

When yeast is used as a leavening agent in bread, it causes the release of carbon dioxide, which makes dough rise. Sourdough bread contains yeast as a natural ingredient derived from airborne yeast spores. Even though labels on commercial sourdough products do not list yeast as an ingredient, it is part of the fermentation process. Because yeast often occurs naturally in certain foods, it may not be mentioned in the label as an added ingredient.

Fresh fruits with thin soft skins may provide a suitable environment for the growth of yeast if stored for long periods *unrefrigerated*. Refrigeration will not completely eliminate the presence of yeast, but it will significantly inhibit its growth. Thick-skinned fruits such as oranges and melons will not readily support the growth of yeast. Fruits in stores frequently contain yeast, and dried fruits invariably contain yeast. Fruit juices do not contain a significant amount of yeast if prepared, covered, refrigerated, and consumed within 24 hours. Quick breads that would ordinarily contain dried fruits are also tasty when made with nuts, ground fresh carrots, or finely chopped zucchini instead.

Some cheeses contain yeast. We have listed common dairy products that have not grown yeast by direct culture on our "safe" list and those that have grown yeast or mold on the "avoid" list. Though our efforts are not exhaustive, enough foods are mentioned to allow for an adequate choice. Remember that absence of yeast growth from a food by direct culture does not completely exclude the possibility of yeast allergen from being present.

Vinegars, because they are the result of yeast fermentation, contain yeast allergen.

Vitamin B is a complex group of vitamins essential for good health. Yeast is a common and inexpensive natural source of Vitamin B and is widely used in foods as a vitamin supplement. Synthetic vitamins of the B complex are free of yeast, though Riboflavin may contain a small amount.

Study the labels of all food to determine if they contain yeast. Prepare foods in containers that have been thoroughly cleaned of any foods containing yeast. Steam or fats that have been used in the preparation of foods containing yeast (such as frying foods in bread crumbs) should not be permitted to come in contact with yeast-free foods under preparation. Do not overlook yeast-containing foods prepared in restaurants and other people's homes. Do not expect restaurant personnel to know what yeast is or where it is present.

## SUBSTITUTIONS

Baker's yeast—baking soda, baking powder
Brewer's yeast—non-alcoholic flavorings may be used in place of wine or liquor in foods; synthetic vitamin B compounds may be substituted for Brewer's yeast when it is used as a dietary supplement.
Vitamins—synthetic vitamins
Vinegar—pure lemon juice

## COOKING HINTS

The importance of baker's yeast in a bread or pastry is to help produce a lighter product. Baking powder and baking soda are also used to cause a product to rise, but are *not* equal to or interchangeable with baker's yeast. Breads and pastries made with baking powder and baking soda may be satisfactorily substituted for the same kinds of products made with baker's yeast, but may vary slightly in taste or texture.

Pure lemon juice can replace equal amounts of vinegar in recipes without altering the taste or quality.

## AVOID THESE GENERAL TYPES OF FOOD IN WHICH YEAST IS USUALLY FOUND

*Baby Foods*
   commercially prepared (some)

*Bakery Products*
   Biscuits
   Breadings

Breads
Cake mixes
Cakes
Cookies
Crackers
Hamburger buns

Hotdog buns
Pastries
Rolls
Stuffings

## Cereals
(some)

## Desserts and Sweets
Candy (some)
Ice-cream flavorings (some)
Malted products

## Beverages
Beer
Brandy
Fruit juices (not freshly squeezed)
Gin
Liquors
Malted milk
Root beer (not artificially
    flavored)
Rum
Vodka
Whiskeys
Wines

## Cheeses
(some)

## Fruits
(some)

## Meats
Breaded fish
Breaded meats
Breaded poultry
Meats with fillers

## Condiments
Barbecue sauce
Catsup
Chili sauce
Chutney
Horseradish
Mayonnaise
Miso sauce
Mustard
Pickles
Salad dressings
Sauerkraut
Soy sauce
Tabasco sauce
Tamari sauce
Tomato sauce (some)

## Soups
Commercially prepared

## Snack Foods
(most)

## Vegetables
(some)

# PRODUCTS CONTAINING YEAST AND TO BE AVOIDED

AK-MAK Crackers                Beer

Birds Eye San Francisco–Style
Frozen Vegetables
Brick cheese
Camembert cheese
Campbell's Products
Beef Consommé
Beef Noodle Soup
Beef Soup
Cream of Mushroom Soup
Noodles and Ground Beef
Soup
Sirloin Burger Soup
Catsup
Cheddar cheese (medium)
Coffee-Mate
*Commercially made bread
*Commercially made coffee
cakes
*Commercially made crackers
*Commercially made doughnuts
and sweet rolls
*Commercially made pastries
*Commercially made rolls and
muffins
Corn Chex
Cranberries (fresh)
Dried fruits
English muffins
Golden Gate Sour Bread
Golden Grain Rice-A-Roni, Beef
flavor
**Gorgonzola cheese
Gouda cheese
Kellogg's Raisin Bran
Kohl's Products
Chicken Soup

Old Fashioned Vegetable
Soup
Onion Soup
Split Pea Soup
Vegetable Beef Soup
Vegetarian Vegetable Soup
La Choy Chow Mein Noodles
Lea & Perrin's Worcestershire
Sauce
Limburger cheese
Manischewitz soup mixes (some)
Miso sauce
Mozzarella cheese
Mrs. Grass Noodle Soup Mix
Mrs. Karl's Enriched Rolls
**Mushrooms (fresh)
Nabisco Premium Saltine
Crackers
Natural Ovens of Manitowoc
Sunney Millet Bread
Ovaltine Drink Mixes
Oven Fry Coating
Parmesan cheese
Pepperidge Farm breads
(most)
Pet Ritz Pie Crust
Post Raisin Bran
Quaker Products
Instant Oatmeal with Bran and
Raisins
Instant Oatmeal with Raisins
and Dates
Instant Oatmeal with Raisins
and Spice
Rice Chex
Ricotta Cheese

Rold Gold Pretzels
**Roquefort cheese
Sara Lee coffee cakes
Shake 'n Bake Coating Mixes
(most)
Shrimp (fresh)
Snyder's of Hanover Old
Fashioned Pretzels
Soy Sauce
Spike seasoning
Stilton cheese
Stokely's Japanese-Style Stir-
Fry Vegetables
Stoned Wheat Thins
Strudel
Tabasco sauce
Tamari sauce
Uncle Ben's Long Grain and
Wild Rice
Vegit seasoning
Vinegar
Wine
Wonder Bread
Worcestershire sauce

*As a general rule, avoid these products.
**These foods grew mold under laboratory conditions, but did not produce yeast.

*Other products containing yeast must be avoided. Read labels carefully, as ingredients may be changed without notice.*

# PRODUCTS FREE OF YEAST AND SAFE TO USE

Angostura Bitters
American Cheese
Baker's German Sweet Choco-
late
Ballard Refrigerator Rolls
Barbara Dee Chocolate Squares
Barbara Dee Fun Peanut
Butter Cremes
Betty Crocker Bacos
Betty Crocker Noodles
Stroganoff
Borden's Eagle Brand Sweetened
Condensed Milk
Bran Cereals without raisins
Buc Wheats
Buttermilk
Cantaloupe
Carnation Evaporated Milk
Carr's Table Water Biscuits
Cheerios, Original
Cheerios, Honey Nut
Cheese (most)
Clams, fresh
Cool Whip
Corn Chex
Corn Tortillas

Cottage Cheese
Country Time Lemonade
Cream Cheese
Crunchola Peanut Butter with Maple & Brown Sugar Bars
Daisy Fresh Margarine
Doritos Tortilla Chips
Durkee's O & C Real French-Fried Onions
Durkee's Pure Vanilla Extract
Egg Noodles
EZ Vanilla Tapioca Pudding
Fearn Soyo Pancake Mix
FFV Ocean Crisps
Flavor Tree Products
    French Onion Crisps with Sesame
    Sesame Chips
    Sesame Sticks
Fritos Corn Chips
Geiser's Natural Potato Chips
Golden Grain Macaroni and Cheese
Golden Grain Rice-A-Roni Chicken Flavor
Graham Crackers
Hostess Crumb Cakes
Hostess Donuts
Jewel Maid Refrigerated Rolls
Jell-O Pudding and Pie Fillings
Jiffy Brownie Mix
Jolly Joan Egg Replacer
Jolly Joan Rice Bran
Jose's Tortillos, Burrito-Style
Kellogg's cereals (most)
Kohl's Products
    Chicken "O" Noodle Soup

Cream of Mushroom Soup
Refrigerator Rolls
La Choy Rice Noodles
Libby's Vegetarian Beans
Manischewitz Lima Bean Barley Soup Mix
Margarines
Matzo (Matzah—Unleavened Bread)
Milk, whole
Murray Butter Cookies
Nabisco Products
    Cookies (some)
    Cracker Meal
    Rice Cakes
    Ritz Crackers
    Triscuits
Nestlé's Butterscotch Morsels
Nestlé's Semi-Sweet Chocolate Chips
Old Time Canned Peeled Tomatoes
Old Time Margarine
On-Cor Giblet Gravy Sliced Turkey
Ore-Ida Hash Browns
Ovaltine
Parein TUC Crackers
Peek Freans English Grahams
Pepperidge Farm Frozen Patty Shells
PET Evaporated Milk
Pillsbury Products
    Danish Refrigerator Rolls
    Enriched white flour
    Hotloaf Refrigerated Bread Dough
    Quick Bread Mixes

Refrigerated Rolls
Piñata Corn Tortillas
Post Corn Tortillas
Post Country Crisp Brown Sugar
  n' Honey Corn Flakes
Postum
Pringle's Potato Chips
Puffed Rice
Puffed Wheat
Quaker Instant Oatmeal
  Apples and Cinnamon
  Maple and Brown Sugar
  Plain
Quaker Old Fashioned Rolled
  Oats
Rice Cakes
Rice Chex
Rice Krispies
Romano Cheese
Root Beer (artificially flavored)
Roundy's Products
  Chop suey vegetables
  Instant non-fat dry milk
  Pitted ripe olives
  Potato chips

Tomato paste
Rye Krisp (natural and seasoned)
Sour cream
Sour Half-and-Half
Stokely's Chinese-Style Stir-Fry
  Vegetables
Stouffer's Products
  Blueberry Crumb Cakes
  Cheese Crumb Cakes
  Cherry Crumb Cakes
  Chocolate Chip Crumb Cakes
  French Crumb Cakes
  Spinach Soufflé
Swift's Brown n' Serve Sausage
Tofu
Van Camp's New Orleans–Style
  Red Kidney Beans
Vanillin
Wasa Bröd Crisp Rye Bread
Wheat Chex
Wheaties
Wheat Tortillas
Whipping Cream
Yogurt

*Read labels carefully, as ingredients may be changed without notice.*

## Yeast-Free Recipes

### *Appetizers / Dips / Spreads*

# 7

# *Recipes for*
# *Appetizers/*
# *Dips/*
# *Spreads*

## ☐ *CHEESE HORS D'OEUVRES*

### PASTRY

2 packages (8 ounces each)
cream cheese, softened
½ pound butter, softened

2¼ cups sifted pure
wheat pastry flour
¼ teaspoon salt

**Free of:**
Corn
Soy
Yeast

### FILLING

1½ pounds Romano cheese,
grated
1 egg beaten

¼ cup chopped parsley
(optional)

Cream the cheese and butter until well blended. To
form dough, gradually add flour and salt until well

blended. Divide into 4 equal balls and wrap each ball in waxed paper. Chill dough in refrigerator for at least 30 minutes. Roll out each ball of dough on lightly floured board to ¼- to ½-inch thick or the thickness of pie crust. Then cut out circles 2½ to 3 inches in diameter.

Combine cheese, egg, and parsley. Place 1 teaspoon of filling on half of each circle; fold over; press edges shut on each side with fork tines. Bake on lightly greased cookie sheet in a preheated 350°F oven 20 minutes, or until golden brown. Serve piping hot.

*Note:* Allow frozen CHEESE HORS D'OEUVRES to thaw 30 minutes before baking.

*Makes about 8 dozen.*

## □ *CHEESE PINWHEELS*

**Free of:**
Corn
Soy
Yeast

**PASTRY**

½ cup butter
1¼ cups sifted pure
   wheat pastry flour
¼ teaspoon salt

1/3 teaspoon corn-free baking
   powder
½ cup sour cream

**FILLING**

1¼ pounds dry cottage cheese
2 eggs

2 teaspoons melted butter
¼ teaspoon salt

Mix filling ingredients together in small bowl until well blended, and set aside. Mix pastry ingredients as for pie dough, cutting butter into mixed dry ingredients, then adding cream. Divide into 4 parts. Wrap in waxed paper and chill 30 minutes to 1 hour. Roll out on floured board into a 9x12-inch rectangle.

Spread cheese filling on dough and roll like a jelly roll. Cut into 2-inch slices, dot each with butter, and bake 2 inches apart on a greased cookie sheet in a preheated 350°F oven for 40 minutes or until golden brown. Serve hot with sour cream and BLUEBERRY SAUCE (page 262) or frozen strawberries.

*Note:* CHEESE PINWHEELS may be frozen unbaked. To serve, put frozen CHEESE PINWHEELS on cookie sheet. Bake in preheated 350°F oven for 40 minutes or more, until golden brown.

*Makes approximately 4 dozen appetizers.*

## □ CHEESE ROLLS

| | | Free of: |
|---|---|---|
| 2 packages (8 ounces each) cream cheese, softened | 1 tablespoon finely chopped pimiento | Corn |
| 2 cups (8 ounces) shredded Romano cheese | dash of salt | Egg |
| | dash of pepper | Soy |
| 1 tablespoon finely chopped onion or green onion | 1 cup CRISPY HERB TOPPING (page 154) | Wheat |
| | | Yeast |

Combine all ingredients except topping, mixing until well blended; chill several hours. Shape to form ball; roll in CRISPY HERB TOPPING, coating well. Chill; serve with crackers or raw vegetables, as desired.

*Makes 10 to 12 servings.*

## □ EGGPLANT SPREAD

| | | Free of: |
|---|---|---|
| | | Corn |
| ¼ cup olive oil | 1 tablespoon lemon juice | Egg |
| 1 medium eggplant (about 1 pound), cut into bite-size chunks | ¾ teaspoon salt | Milk |
| | ½ teaspoon basil | Soy |
| ½ cup water | ¼ teaspoon cracked pepper | Wheat |
| ½ cup lightly packed parsley | | Yeast |

About 1½ hours before serving or day ahead:

In 12-inch skillet over medium heat, in hot olive oil, cook eggplant 5 minutes, stirring constantly. Add water; reduce heat to low; cover and simmer about 10 minutes or until eggplant is tender, stirring occasionally.

Place eggplant, parsley, and remaining ingredients in blender container; cover blender; blend at high speed until eggplant is chopped, scraping blender container with rubber spatula occasionally. Spoon mixture into medium bowl; cover and refrigerate.

To serve, let each person spread some eggplant on RyKrisp.

*Makes about 2 cups spread, or 32 appetizer servings.*

## □ *LUAU CHUNKS*

**Free of:**

Corn

Egg

Milk

Soy

Wheat

Yeast

2 tablespoons brown sugar
2 tablespoons potato starch
¼ teaspoon salt
¼ teaspoon powdered ginger
1 can (1 pound 14 ounces)
  pineapple chunks in
  own juice

water
½ cup apple juice
2 pounds precooked beef
  or ham, cut in
  1-inch cubes

In saucepan combine brown sugar, potato starch, salt, and ginger. Drain pineapple, reserving juice. Add enough water to pineapple juice to make 1½ cups; put into saucepan. Stir in apple juice and cook over medium heat, stirring constantly, until sauce boils and thickens. (Refrigerate the sauce if you are preparing in advance.) Pour into chafing dish or electric skillet to keep warm. Add pineapple chunks and heat half of the meat cubes at one time (takes about 5 minutes). More may be added later. Use toothpicks for serving pineapple.

*Makes about 80 appetizers.*

# □ *PEANUT BUTTER CRUNCHY SPREAD*

1¼ cups natural peanut butter    ½ cup honey
2/3 cup toasted oats

**Free of:**
Corn
Egg
Milk
Soy
Wheat
Yeast

Combine all ingredients; mix well. Store in tightly covered container in refrigerator. Serve as sandwich spread, on celery and carrot sticks, or on apple and pear slices.

*Makes about 1¾ cups spread.*

# □ *PEANUT BUTTER ENRICHED SPREAD*

water
1/3 cup dry milk powder (½ cup)
1 cup natural peanut butter

2–3 tablespoons soft butter or
   safflower oil
3 tablespoons honey (optional)

**Free of:**
Corn
Egg
Soy
Wheat
Yeast

Add a few drops of water to dry milk powder and stir into a smooth paste. Blend it into the peanut butter with a knife; then blend in the butter or oil and honey.

Use this spread in place of regular peanut butter for sandwiches. Try stuffing celery stalks with it for snacks.

*Makes about 1¼ cups spread.*

## □ *RAMAKI*

**Free of:** ½ pound chicken livers, fresh or    1 cup apple juice
Corn      frozen                       ¼ cup pure beef broth
Egg      2 tablespoons safflower oil     ¼ cup water
Milk     2 cans (5 ounces each) water    ½ teaspoon powdered ginger
Soy        chestnuts
Wheat   ½ pound sliced beef bacon
Yeast

    Cook chicken livers slowly in safflower oil for 5 minutes; cut into quarters. Slice water chestnuts into 2 pieces. Cut each bacon strip across in half and wrap around liver and water-chestnut pieces; secure with toothpick. Prepare sauce by combining apple juice with beef broth, water, and ginger; marinate bacon wrap-ups in mixture for at least 1 hour. Broil about 3 inches from source of heat, turning as necessary, until browned.

*Makes about 36 appetizers.*

## □ *TOFU SPREAD*

**Free of:** 6 ounces tofu (bean-curd cheese)    1 tablespoon lemon juice
Corn      ¼ cup natural peanut butter     1 tablespoon honey
Egg      1 small banana
Milk
Wheat      Combine ingredients in blender; puree until smooth.
Yeast    Serve as is on wheat-free bread or crackers. May be topped with nuts or thinly sliced bananas. Also delicious frozen until firm, stirred (to break up crystals), refrozen, and served as rich sherbet.

*Makes approximately 1 cup of spread.*

# Recipes for
# Beverages

## ☐ *CAROB MILK*

1 tablespoon roasted carob powder    1 cup milk, hot or cold
1 tablespoon honey

**Free of:**
Corn
Egg
Soy
Wheat
Yeast

Combine ingredients in a large glass.

## □ *CITRUS SPARKLER*

**Free of:**
Corn
Egg
Milk
Soy
Wheat
Yeast

1 can (12-ounce) frozen orange-
  juice concentrate
30 ounces water
2 tablespoons lime juice
4 teaspoons artificial rum
  flavoring

1 bottle (32-ounce) chilled sugar-
  free lemon-lime carbonated
  beverage
2 limes, sliced
ice cubes

About 10 minutes before serving, in large pitcher, stir until well mixed undiluted orange-juice concentrate, 2½ juice cans cold water, lime juice, and rum flavoring. Add carbonated beverage and lime slices.

To serve, stir punch well; pour over ice cubes in tall glass.

*Makes about 9 cups, or 12 6-ounce servings.*

## □ *COUNTERFEIT COCKTAIL*

**Free of:**
Corn
Egg
Milk
Soy
Wheat
Yeast

1 tall glass soda water
½ fresh lime

Angostura bitters

Pour soda water over ice in a tall glass. Add juice of ½ lime and a dash of bitters. Stir and serve.

**Free of:**
Corn
Egg
Milk
Soy
Wheat
Yeast

## □ *SALTY DOG*

2 cups freshly squeezed grapefruit juice
kosher salt

1 tray ice cubes

Squeeze the grapefruit juice. (Canned or frozen juice will do, but fresh is best.) Rub the rims of 4 glasses with juice; then dip each one in a plate of kosher salt. Fill each glass with ice cubes and pour grapefruit juice over the ice.

## □ *SPICE-AMATO*

1 teaspoon fresh lime juice
¼ teaspoon plain salt
dash ground pepper

1 cup V-8 or tomato juice
dash Tabasco sauce

**Free of:**
Corn
Egg
Milk
Soy
Wheat

In a pitcher, mix lime juice, salt, and pepper until salt is dissolved. Add V-8 juice or tomato juice and mix. Add Tabasco sauce. Pour over ice in a tall glass and garnish with a celery stick to stir.

# Recipes for Breads / Biscuits / Crackers / Muffins / Quick Breads/ Yeast Breads

## □ BAKING POWDER BISCUITS #1

2 cups pure wheat
  pastry flour
1 tablespoon corn-free
  baking powder

1 teaspoon salt
¼ cup butter
¾ cup milk

**Free of:**
Corn
Egg
Soy
Yeast

    In large bowl, combine dry ingredients. Add butter and cut in until mixture resembles coarse crumbs. With fork, quickly mix in milk just until mixture forms soft dough that leaves the side of the bowl. Turn dough onto floured board; knead one minute to mix thoroughly. Roll dough evenly ¼- to ½-inch thick. With sharp knife, cut 2x2-inch diamonds, using straight, downward motion. With pancake turner, place diamonds on ungreased cookie sheet

1 inch apart. Press trimmings together; roll and cut until all dough is used. Bake at 450°F for 12 to 15 minutes, until golden.

*Makes 15 biscuits.*

## □ *BAKING POWDER BISCUITS #2*

**Free of:**
Corn
Egg
Soy
Wheat
Yeast

⅝ cup potato-starch flour
2 teaspoons corn-free
    baking powder

¼ teaspoon salt
3 tablespoons butter
¼ cup milk

In medium mixing bowl, sift together potato-starch flour, baking powder, and salt. Cut in butter until all butter is evenly combined with flour. Stir in milk to make a soft dough. Round up on lightly floured (potato-starch flour) board. Knead lightly. Roll out about ½-inch thick. Cut and place on ungreased baking sheet.
    Bake in 500°F oven for 10 minutes, until golden brown. Serve piping hot.

*Makes 8 to 10 biscuits.*

## □ *BANANA BISCUITS*

**Free of:**
Corn
Egg
Milk
Soy
Wheat
Yeast

1 cup rice flour
2 teaspoons corn-free
    baking powder
¼ teaspoon salt

1½ teaspoons sugar
2 tablespoon safflower oil
½ cup mashed ripe banana
1/3 cup water

In medium bowl, combine rice flour, baking powder, salt, and sugar. Add oil and cut in until consistency of coarse meal. Add banana and water; mix thoroughly. Form into a cylinder and cut biscuits. Place biscuits, touching one another, on a greased cookie sheet.

Bake in a preheated 400°F oven for 20 to 25 minutes, or until lightly browned.

*Makes 8 biscuits.*

## □ OAT-AND-HONEY BISCUITS

| | | |
|---|---|---|
| 1 cup oat flour | 1½ tablespoons safflower oil | **Free of:** |
| 2½ teaspoons corn-free | 1 tablespoon honey | Corn |
| baking powder | ¼ cup water | Egg |
| ¼ teaspoon salt | | Milk |
| | | Soy |
| | | Wheat |
| | | Yeast |

Into small bowl, sift oat flour, and then measure 1 cup. Into another bowl, put oat flour and add baking powder and salt. Stir oil and honey together and cut into flour mixture until crumbly. Add water to make a soft dough; if necessary, add an additional teaspoon or so of water to get desired consistency. Form dough into small biscuits and place on a greased cookie sheet.

Bake in a preheated hot 450°F oven for 15 to 20 minutes.

*Makes 8 biscuits.*

## □ POTATO BISCUITS

| | | |
|---|---|---|
| ⅝ cup potato flour | 2 tablespoons safflower oil | **Free of:** |
| 3 teaspoons corn-free | 1 cup mashed potatoes | Corn |
| baking powder | ½ cup water | Egg |
| 1 teaspoon salt | | Milk |
| | | Soy |
| | | Wheat |
| | | Yeast |

In medium bowl, sift together flour, baking powder, and salt. Cut in oil. Add potato; mix thoroughly. Add enough water to make a soft dough. Roll dough on a floured board to about a ½-inch thickness. Cut into biscuits.

Bake on greased cookie sheet at 400°F for 12 to 15 minutes.

*Makes 8 biscuits.*

## □ CARAWAY-RYE CRACKERS

**Free of:**
Corn
Egg
Milk
Soy
Yeast

1 1/3 cups sifted pure wheat pastry flour
2/3 cup rye flour
1/3 cup safflower oil
1½ teaspoons caraway seed

1 teaspoon salt
½ teaspoon baking soda
2 tablespoons lemon juice
¼ cup water

In medium bowl, measure all ingredients. Stir until well mixed and dough forms a ball. On lightly floured board, roll one half of dough 1/16-inch thick. Cut 3½-inch circles with a cookie cutter. With spatula, put circles on ungreased cookie sheets. Prick circles several times with a fork. Repeat until all dough is used.

Bake at 375°F for 12 to 15 minutes, until golden. Cool on racks. Store in tightly covered container.

*Makes about 24 crackers.*

**Free of:**
Corn
Egg
Milk
Soy
Wheat
Yeast

## □ HERB CRISPS

2 tablespoons safflower oil
¼ teaspoon basil
¼ teaspoon thyme

¼ teaspoon ginger
¼ teaspoon celery salt
12 RyKrisp crackers

In small bowl, mix oil with seasonings. Spread RyKrisp crackers with seasoned oil. Place in shallow pan. Bake for 5 minutes at 350°F.

Serve warm or cold.

## □ *WHOLE-WHEAT WAFERS*

| | | |
|---|---|---|
| *1½ cups sifted whole-wheat flour* | *dill seeds (optional)* | **Free of:** |
| *1 teaspoon salt* | *sesame seeds (optional)* | *Corn* |
| *½ cup yogurt* | | *Egg* |
| | | *Soy* |
| | | *Yeast* |

In small bowl, blend flour and salt. Gradually work in yogurt to make dough. Knead on lightly floured board for about 15 to 20 minutes. Roll thin and cut into cracker shapes. Prick with a fork. Sprinkle lightly with dill seed or sesame seed.

Bake 10 minutes, until lightly brown, at 350°F.

*Makes approximately 12 wafers, depending on the size and shape desired.*

## □ *BARLEY MUFFINS*

| | | |
|---|---|---|
| *1½ cups barley flour* | *½ teaspoon salt* | **Free of:** |
| *½ cup rice flour* | *1 cup water* | *Corn* |
| *¼ cup light-brown sugar* | *¼ cup safflower oil* | *Egg* |
| *4 teaspoons corn-free* | | *Milk* |
| *baking powder* | | *Soy* |
| | | *Wheat* |
| | | *Yeast* |

Combine barley flour, rice flour, sugar, baking powder, and salt in a bowl. Add water and oil; mix well. Fill greased muffin tins about half full.

Bake in a preheated 375°F oven for 25 minutes, or until lightly browned.

*Makes 1 dozen muffins.*

## □ BASIC MUFFINS

**Free of:**
Corn
Egg
Soy
Yeast

2 cups sifted pure wheat
   pastry flour
2½ teaspoons corn-free baking
   powder
2 tablespoons sugar
¾ teaspoon salt

1 teaspoon powdered egg
   replacer
2 tablespoons water
¾ cup milk
¼ cup safflower oil

Sift flour, baking powder, sugar, and salt together into a medium bowl. In small bowl, blend together egg replacer and water, and combine with milk and oil. Add liquid mixture all at once to flour mixture. Stir until dry ingredients are thoroughly dampened. Turn into greased muffin pans about 2/3 full.

Bake at 400°F for 25 minutes, or until done.

**Variations:** 1 cup fresh frozen blueberries may be added, or ½ cup crushed crisp bacon.

*Makes 10 muffins.*

## □ BLUEBERRY MUFFINS #1

**Free of:**
Corn
Soy
Yeast

2 cups sifted pure wheat
   pastry flour
3 teaspoons corn-free baking
   powder
3 tablespoons sugar
1 teaspoon salt

1 egg, slightly beaten
1 cup milk
¼ cup safflower oil
1 cup fresh blueberries

Heat oven to 400°F. Sift flour, baking powder, sugar, and salt into medium-size mixing bowl. Make a well in middle of dry ingredients and add egg, milk, and oil. Mix thoroughly, only enough to moisten the dry ingredients.

Fold in blueberries. Fill greased muffin cups 2/3 full with batter.
Bake 20 to 25 minutes.

*Makes about 12 muffins.*

## □ BLUEBERRY MUFFINS #2

| | | Free of: |
|---|---|---|
| 3 tablespoons butter | 1½ cups fresh or frozen blue- | **Free of:** |
| 2 cups rice flour | berries | Corn |
| 4 teaspoons corn-free baking | 2 eggs, beaten | Soy |
| powder | 1¼ cups milk | Wheat |
| ½ cup sugar | 1 teaspoon pure vanilla extract | Yeast |
| 1 teaspoon salt | | |

Set oven to 400°F. Melt butter in large cooking pot. Set aside and allow to cool. Sift flour, baking powder, sugar, and salt together into a medium bowl. Mix berries with ¼ of this mixture. Add eggs, milk, and vanilla to cooled butter, and beat well. Stir dry ingredients into egg mixture, just enough to combine. Fold in blueberries, stirring gently. Line muffin tins with paper liners; fill paper muffin-tin liners ¾ full.
Bake in 400°F oven for 25 minutes, or until tops of muffins are nicely browned.

*Makes 12 large muffins.*

## □ BRAN MUFFINS #1

| | | Free of: |
|---|---|---|
| 1½ cups bran-flake cereal | 3 teaspoons corn-free baking | **Free of:** |
| 1 cup water | powder | Corn |
| 1 egg | ½ teaspoon salt | Milk |
| ¼ cup safflower oil | 1/3 cup sugar | Soy |
| 1¼ cups pure wheat pastry | | Yeast |
| flour, sifted | | |

Measure bran and water into large mixing bowl. Stir until combined. Let stand 2 minutes or until cereal is softened. Add egg and oil. Beat well. Add dry ingredients to cereal mixture, stirring only until combined. Portion batter evenly into 12 greased 2½-inch muffin-pan cups.

Bake in oven at 400°F about 25 minutes or until muffins are golden brown. Serve hot.

*Makes 12 muffins.*

## □ *BRAN MUFFINS #2*

**Free of:**

| | | |
|---|---|---|
| Corn | 1½ cups unprocessed wheat bran | ¾ cup buttermilk |
| Corn | 1 cup whole-wheat flour | ½ cup molasses |
| Soy | 1 teaspoon baking soda | 2 tablespoons safflower oil |
| Yeast | 2 teaspoons corn-free baking powder | 1 egg, beaten |

Stir together bran, flour, soda, and baking powder in large bowl. Set aside. In medium bowl, blend buttermilk, molasses, oil, and egg; add to dry ingredients and stir just until moistened. Fill oiled muffin cups 2/3 full.

Bake 15 to 20 minutes in 400°F oven.

*Makes 12 muffins.*

## □ *CORN MUFFINS*

**Free of:**

| | | |
|---|---|---|
| Soy | 1 cup corn flour | 1 egg |
| Wheat | 1 cup potato starch | ¼ cup butter, soft |
| Wheat | 2 tablespoons baking powder | ¾ cup milk |
| Yeast | ¼ teaspoon salt | |

Sift dry ingredients into large bowl and set aside. In another, medium bowl, cream egg and butter. Stir in milk and add mixture to dry ingredients. Line muffin tins with paper liners; fill paper muffin-tin liners ¾ full. Bake at 350°F for 30 minutes or until done.

*Makes 12 rolls.*

## □ EGGLESS MUFFINS

| | | |
|---|---|---|
| 1½ cups unsifted pure wheat pastry flour | 1 cup buttermilk | **Free of:** |
| 3 tablespoons sugar | 3 tablespoons safflower oil | Corn |
| ½ teaspoon baking soda | Jelly or jam (made without corn syrup or corn sweetener) | Egg |
| ½ teaspoon salt | | Soy |
| | | Yeast |

In a medium bowl, thoroughly mix flour, sugar, baking soda, and salt. Add buttermilk and safflower oil and stir just until dry ingredients are moistened. Fill greased medium-size muffin cups about 1/3 full. Place 1 teaspoon jelly or jam in the center of each; then fill cups about 2/3 full with remaining batter.

Bake at 400°F for 25 minutes or until done. Immediately remove from muffin cups; serve hot.

*Makes 1 dozen muffins.*

## □ ENGLISH BRAN MUFFINS

| | | |
|---|---|---|
| 1 package dry yeast, dissolved in ¼ cup lukewarm water | 1 heaping cup unprocessed wheat bran | **Free of:** |
| 1 cup very warm water | 2 cups whole-wheat flour | Corn |
| 1 teaspoon salt | 2 cups unbleached white flour | Egg |
| 2 teaspoons honey (optional) | 3 tablespoons safflower oil | Milk |
| | | Soy |

Combine the dissolved yeast, water, salt, honey, and bran in a large bowl. Mix the flours together in a separate bowl, and gradually beat half of the flour into the bran mixture. Cover the bowl and allow to rise in a warm place for 1½ hours. Beat in the oil and add the rest of the flour, reserving ½ cup for the board. Turn out onto the board and knead until smooth. Don't skimp on the kneading. Pat the dough out, spreading until it's about ¾-inch thick. Cut into 3-inch rounds; cover on the board for about 1 hour.

Cook at a preheated 300°F in an electric fry pan or on the griddle of your stove, lightly oiled, for 12 or 13 minutes, turning once. If you don't have either of these, use an iron griddle.

To serve, split and toast.

*Makes approximately 24 muffins.*


## □ *ONION MUFFINS*

**Free of:**
Corn
Milk
Soy
Wheat
Yeast

4 eggs, separated
1 tablespoon light-brown sugar
¼ teaspoon salt
2 tablespoons cold water

½ cup potato starch
1 teaspoon corn-free baking powder
½ teaspoon onion powder

In small bowl, beat egg whites until stiff peaks form; set aside. In medium bowl, beat egg yolks until lemon-colored. Add sugar, salt, and cold water. Sift together potato starch, baking powder, and onion powder; add gradually to egg yolks. Fold into egg whites. Fill greased muffin tin.

Bake in a preheated 350°F oven for 15 to 20 minutes or until lightly browned.

*Makes 8 servings.*

## □ QUICK BRAN MUFFINS

3 cups unprocessed wheat bran　　2½ cups pure wheat
1 cup boiling water　　　　　　　　　pastry flour
1 cup brown sugar　　　　　　　　2½ teaspoons baking soda
½ cup safflower or sunflower oil　1 teaspoon salt
2 eggs　　　　　　　　　　　　　　1 pint buttermilk

**Free of:**
Corn
Soy
Yeast

In large bowl, combine 1 cup bran and 1 cup boiling water; stir and let steep. In a separate bowl, cream sugar and oil. Add eggs one at a time and beat. Combine the 1 cup of steeped bran with remaining two cups of bran and with the eggs, flour, soda, salt, buttermilk, oil, and sugar. Mix very well. Store in tightly covered plastic container. Let stand at least 12 hours before baking. Batter will keep in refrigerator for 6 weeks.

These muffins are mixed, stored in the refrigerator, and baked whenever they are wanted. Twenty-five minutes before serving, preheat oven to 400°F. Spoon batter into buttered muffin tins, filling 2/3 full. Bake 20 to 22 minutes and serve. You can make only 2 muffins or enough for a large family.

## □ RYE MUFFINS #1

1 cup medium rye flour　　　　　¼ teaspoon salt
2 tablespoons sugar　　　　　　½ cup water
2 teaspoons corn-free baking　　2 tablespoons safflower oil
　powder

**Free of:**
Corn
Egg
Milk
Soy
Wheat
Yeast

About 45 minutes before serving:
Preheat oven to 400°F. Grease 6 2½-inch muffin-pan cups.

In medium bowl, with fork, mix first 4 ingredients. Add water and safflower oil, stirring just until moistened. (Batter will be lumpy.)

Spoon batter into muffin-pan cups. Bake 30 to 35 minutes, until muffins come away from edges of pan.

## Variations:

**Cinnamon-Raisin Muffins:** Prepare RYE MUFFINS as directed, but stir ½ cup raisins and ½ teaspoon ground cinnamon into dry ingredients. (This variation is not yeast-free.)

**Nut Muffins:** Prepare RYE MUFFINS as directed, but add ½ cup chopped nuts to dry ingredients.

*Makes 6 muffins.*

## □ RYE MUFFINS #2

**Free of:**
Corn
Egg
Milk
Soy
Wheat
Yeast

1¼ cups rye flour
½ cup potato flour
¼ cup light-brown sugar
4 teaspoons corn-free baking
   powder

½ teaspoon salt
1 cup water
¼ cup safflower oil

Combine rye flour, potato flour, sugar, baking powder, and salt in a bowl. Add water and oil; mix well. Fill greased muffin tins about half full.

Bake in a preheated 375°F oven for 25 minutes or until lightly browned.

*Makes 1 dozen muffins.*

## □ *BANANA BREAD #1*

| | | |
|---|---|---|
| ½ cup safflower oil | 2 cups sifted pure wheat | **Free of:** |
| 1 cup sugar | pastry flour | Corn |
| 2 eggs | 1 teaspoon salt | Milk |
| 2 mashed bananas, not overripe | 1 teaspoon baking soda | Soy |
| | ¼ cup chopped nonroasted nuts | Yeast |

Cream oil and sugar in large mixing bowl. Add eggs one at a time and beat well. Add bananas, then remaining ingredients, and beat well.

Bake in 9x5-inch loaf pan (greased if not Teflon-coated) at 350°F for 50 to 60 minutes or until a toothpick comes out clean.

*Makes 1 loaf.*

## □ *BANANA BREAD #2*

| | | |
|---|---|---|
| 2 cups sifted pure wheat | 2/3 cup sugar | **Free of:** |
| pastry flour | 1/3 cup safflower oil | Corn |
| 2 teaspoons corn-free baking | 1 cup mashed ripe bananas | Egg |
| powder | (about 2 large) | Milk |
| ½ teaspoon salt | | Soy |
| ¼ teaspoon baking soda | | Yeast |

About 3 hours before serving or day ahead:

Preheat oven to 350°F. Grease 9x5–inch loaf pan. In medium bowl, with fork, mix well first 4 ingredients; set aside. In large bowl with mixer at medium speed, beat sugar and oil until creamy and smooth, about 5 minutes, scraping bowl occasionally with rubber spatula. Reduce speed to low; alternately add flour mixture and bananas, beating just until smooth. (Dough will be thick and stick to beaters.) Evenly spoon mixture into pan.

Bake 50 minutes or until a toothpick inserted in center comes out clean. Cool in pan on wire rack 10 minutes; remove from pan and cool completely on rack. To store, cover with plastic wrap and refrigerate.

*Makes 1 loaf.*


## □ *BANANA-NUT BREAD #1*

**Free of:**

| | | |
|---|---|---|
| Corn | 1½ cups rice flour | ½ teaspoon salt |
| Milk | 1 cup potato starch | 2 eggs, beaten |
| Soy | 1 tablespoon corn-free baking | ½ cup safflower oil |
| Wheat | powder | 2 tablespoons water |
| Yeast | 1 1/3 cups mashed bananas | ¼ cup coarsely chopped, |
| | ¼ cup light-brown sugar | nonroasted walnuts |

In small bowl, sift together rice flour, potato starch, and baking powder. In a large bowl, combine mashed banana, sugar, and salt; add beaten eggs, oil, and water. Mix well. Stir in dry ingredients. Add nuts. Pour into a greased 8x4–inch loaf pan. Let stand at room temperature for 5 minutes before placing in oven.

Bake in a preheated 350°F oven for 1 hour. Remove from pan onto a rack to cool.

*Makes 8 servings.*


## □ *BANANA-NUT BREAD #2*

**Free of:**

| | | |
|---|---|---|
| Corn | 1 cup rice flour | 1/3 cup safflower oil |
| Milk | ¾ teaspoon baking soda | 2 eggs |
| Soy | 1¼ teaspoons cream of tartar | 1½ cups mashed bananas |
| Wheat | ½ teaspoon salt | ½ cup chopped nuts |
| Yeast | 2/3 cup sugar | |

Sift the flour, soda, cream of tartar, and salt together in large bowl. Gradually add the sugar and the oil, beating until light and fluffy. Add the eggs, one at a time, and beat well. Add the mashed banana (a small amount at a time), beating after each addition until smooth. Add chopped nuts. Mix well.

Pour into a well-greased loaf pan and bake for 1 hour at 350°F.

## □ BRAN BREAD

| | | Free of: |
|---|---|---|
| 1½ cups pure wheat pastry flour | ¼ cup safflower oil | Corn |
| ½ cup sugar | 1½ cups unprocessed wheat bran | Milk |
| 1 teaspoon baking soda | 1½ cups hot water | Soy |
| 1 teaspoon corn-free baking powder | 1 egg | Yeast |
| 1 teaspoon salt | 1 teaspoon pure vanilla extract | |
| | ¾ cup chopped, nonroasted nuts | |

In small bowl, stir together flour, baking powder, soda, and salt. Combine in large bowl bran, oil, and hot water. Mix well. Add egg and vanilla. Beat well. Add the mixed dry ingredients and stir just until all the dry ingredients are moistened.

Spread mixed batter in an oiled loaf pan and bake at 375°F for 60 minutes. Cool before slicing.

**Variation:**  If 1 cup raisins is added, recipe *contains* yeast.

## □ CORN BREAD #1

| | | Free of: |
|---|---|---|
| 2 cups yellow cornmeal | 1 egg | Milk |
| 2 tablespoons sugar | 1 cup water | Soy |
| 1 tablespoon baking powder | ¼ cup safflower oil | Wheat |
| 1 teaspoon salt | | Yeast |

About 35 minutes before serving:

Preheat oven to 425°F. Grease 8x8–inch baking pan. In medium bowl, with fork, mix first 4 ingredients. In small bowl, with fork, mix well egg, water, and safflower oil; pour all at once into cornmeal mixture, stirring just until moistened. Quickly pour batter into baking pan, spreading evenly.

Bake 25 minutes or until golden.

*Makes 12 servings.*


## □ *CORN BREAD #2*

**Free of:**
Soy
Wheat
Yeast

| | |
|---|---|
| 1 cup cornmeal | 2 eggs |
| 2 tablespoons sugar | ½ cup milk |
| ¼ teaspoon salt | 2 tablespoons corn oil |
| 2 teaspoons baking powder | |

Mix dry ingredients in medium mixing bowl. Add to dry ingredients eggs, milk, and oil, all at once, and blend well. Pour into greased 8x8–inch pan. Bake in 425°F oven for 20 to 25 minutes.

*Makes 16 2-inch squares.*


## □ *CRANBERRY BREAD*

**Free of:**
Corn
Milk
Soy

| | |
|---|---|
| 2 cups sifted pure wheat pastry flour | 1 teaspoon grated orange peel |
| 1 cup sugar | ¾ cup orange juice |
| 1½ teaspoons salt | 1 well-beaten egg |
| ½ teaspoon baking soda | 1 cup fresh cranberries, chopped |
| ¼ cup safflower oil | ½ cup nonroasted nuts, chopped |

In large bowl, sift together first 4 ingredients. Cut in oil. Add peel, juice, and egg, mixing just to moisten. Fold in berries and nuts.

Bake in 9x5–inch greased loaf pan at 350°F for 60 minutes. Cool. Wrap in airtight wrap; refrigerate or freeze.

## □ DATE-BRAN BREAD

2 cups boiling water
¾ pound dates, sliced
2 large eggs
¾ cup sugar or honey
1½ cups whole-wheat flour
2 cups unbleached flour
1 teaspoon pure vanilla extract

2 teaspoons corn-free baking powder
1 teaspoon baking soda
2 cups unprocessed wheat bran
1 cup nonroasted chopped nuts
¼ teaspoon salt

**Free of:**
Corn
Milk
Soy

In small bowl, pour boiling water over dates and let cool. In large bowl, beat eggs until light and thick. Slowly beat in sugar or honey until mixture makes a rope when dropped from beaters. Stir the whole-wheat flour into the egg mixture. Fold in half the dates, half the soaking water, the unbleached flour, and vanilla. Stir in remaining dry ingredients, remaining dates and water, and the bran, nuts, and salt. Turn mixture into a square 10-inch pan with bottom buttered and floured.

Bake at 375°F for 50 minutes before turning out.

*Makes 12 to 16 servings.*

## □ DUTCH APPLE BREAD

½ cup safflower oil
1 cup sugar
2 eggs
2 cups unsifted pure wheat pastry flour
½ teaspoon baking soda

1/3 cup orange juice
1 teaspoon pure vanilla extract
2 medium apples, peeled and sliced
1/3 cup nonroasted chopped nuts

**Free of:**
Corn
Milk
Soy
Yeast

Cream oil and sugar in large mixing bowl. Add eggs one at a time; beat well. Add vanilla. Add dry ingredients alternately with juice, ending with dry ingredients. Peel, core, and chop apples and add apples and nuts to batter; mix well. Bake in 9x5-inch loaf pan (greased if not Teflon-coated) at 350°F for 40 to 50 minutes or until a toothpick comes out clean.

*Makes 1 loaf.*

## □ NO-YEAST DOUGH BREAD

**Free of:**
Corn
Egg
Soy
Yeast

2 cups pure wheat pastry
 flour
2 teaspoons salt
1 teaspoon baking soda
1 teaspoon corn-free baking
 powder

2 tablespoons brown sugar
½ cup buttermilk
3 tablespoons safflower oil

In large bowl, sift together dry ingredients. Add wet ingredients; this will give a stiff dough. If dough is not stiff, add a bit of flour. Shape into round loaves. Put in greased pie pans. Slit tops.
Bake at 375°F for 55 minutes. Cut when cool.

*Makes 2 loaves.*

## □ NUT BREAD

**Free of:**
Corn
Soy
Yeast

¾ cup sugar
2 tablespoons safflower oil
1 egg
1½ cups milk
3 cups sifted pure wheat
 pastry flour

3½ teaspoons corn-free baking
 powder
1 teaspoon salt
¾ cup chopped nuts, nonroasted

In large bowl, mix sugar, oil, and egg thoroughly. Add milk and stir in dry ingredients; blend in nuts. Pour into greased 9x5–inch loaf pan. Bake at 350°F for 60 to 70 minutes or until a toothpick comes out clean. Crack in top of loaf is characteristic. Cool thoroughly before slicing.

*Makes 1 loaf.*

## □ OATMEAL BREAD

| | | Free of: |
|---|---|---|
| 1 cup rolled oats | ¼ teaspoon cinnamon | Corn |
| ½ cup potato-starch flour | 2 eggs | Milk |
| 2 teaspoons corn-free baking powder | ¼ cup light-brown sugar | Soy |
| ¼ teaspoon baking soda | ¼ cup unsulfured molasses | Wheat |
| ¼ teaspoon salt | 2 tablespoons sesame oil | Yeast |
| ¼ teaspoon ginger | ¼ cup chopped nuts, nonroasted | |

In medium bowl, combine rolled oats, potato-starch flour, baking powder, baking soda, salt, nuts, ginger, and cinnamon; mix well. In a large bowl, beat eggs; add sugar, molasses, and oil. Gradually add the dry mixture and stir well. If batter is too stiff, add 1 to 2 tablespoons water. Pour into a greased 8x4–inch loaf pan.
Bake in a 375°F oven for 25 minutes.

*Makes 8 servings.*

## □ RICE-HERB BREAD

| | | Free of: |
|---|---|---|
| 2 cups rice flour | 2 tablespoons chopped chives | Corn |
| ¼ cup potato starch | 1 tablespoon sugar | Soy |
| ½ cup nonfat dry milk powder | 1 teaspoon salt | Wheat |
| 3 tablespoons corn-free baking powder | 2 eggs | Yeast |
| 2 tablespoons chopped parsley | 1/3 cup safflower oil | |
| | 2 tablespoons water | |

In large bowl, combine rice flour, potato starch, dry milk powder, baking powder, parsley, chives, sugar, and salt. In a medium bowl, beat together eggs, oil, and water. Add to dry mixture and stir until just blended. Pour into a greased 8x3–inch loaf pan. Let stand for 5 minutes before placing in oven.

Bake in a preheated 350°F oven for 1 hour. Remove from pan and cool on a rack. Can be stored in a plastic bag in the refrigerator for several days.

*Makes 16 slices.*

## □ WHOLE-WHEAT QUICK BREAD

**Free of:**
Corn
Soy
Yeast

2 eggs
1 cup honey
¼ cup safflower oil
1½ cup whole-wheat flour
½ cup rolled oats
4 teaspoons corn-free baking powder

½ teaspoon salt
¼ cup raw wheat germ
½ cup milk
¼ cup nonroasted chopped nuts (optional)

In large bowl, beat eggs; add honey and oil. Beat well. Add dry ingredients and milk; mix well. Add nuts; mix.

Bake in 9x5–inch greased loaf pan 350°F for 45 minutes or until a toothpick comes out clean.

*Makes 1 loaf.*

## □ ALMOND ROLLS

**Free of:**
Corn
Egg
Soy
Wheat
Yeast

4 ounces blanched almonds
confectioners' sugar, corn-free
almond extract
3 tablespoons water
⅝ cup potato-starch flour

1 1/3 cups ground rolled oats
1 tablespoon corn-free baking powder
½ teaspoon salt
6 tablespoons butter
¾ cup milk

## FROSTING

*Mix together until smooth:*
*¾ cup confectioners' sugar,*      *3 to 4 tablespoons water*
  *corn-free*

In small bowl, place finely ground almonds, ½ cup confectioners' sugar, ½ teaspoon almond extract, and 3 tablespoons water; mix and set aside.

In large bowl, combine flour, sugar, baking powder, and salt. Cut in butter with fork until mixture resembles coarse crumbs. Add rolled oats, then add milk and ¼ teaspoon almond extract. Mix quickly until dough leaves the side of the bowl.

Knead dough on a floured board for 1 minute. Roll into a 18x18–inch rectangle. Spread with almond mixture to ½ inch of edges. Roll the dough jelly-roll fashion, starting with the 18-inch side. Cut roll into 1-inch slices. Place cut side on greased cookie sheet.

Bake at 400°F for 15 to 18 minutes. Frost while on cookie sheet. Serve warm.

*Makes 18 1-inch rolls.*

## □ BLUEBERRY COFFEE CAKE

| | | Free of: |
|---|---|---|
| ¼ cup butter | ½ cup milk | |
| ¾ cup sugar | 2 cups fresh or frozen | Corn |
| 1 egg | blueberries | Soy |
| 1¼ cups potato-starch flour | 1 teaspoon pure vanilla extract | Wheat |
| 2 teaspoons corn-free baking | | Yeast |
| powder | | |

## TOPPING

| | |
|---|---|
| 3 tablespoons softened butter | ¼ cup potato-starch flour |
| ½ cup sugar | 1 teaspoon cinnamon |

Cream butter and sugar in medium-size mixing bowl. Add egg and vanilla and beat well. Add dry ingredients, then milk, and mix thoroughly. Fold in blueberries. Pour batter into greased 10x10–inch pan.

Combine topping ingredients in small bowl. Sprinkle evenly over top of batter. Bake at 375°F for 40 minutes or until a toothpick comes out clean.

## □ CINNAMON ROLLS

**Free of:**
Corn
Egg
Milk
Soy
Yeast

### FILLING

½ cup brown sugar
½ cup nonroasted chopped nuts

1½ teaspoons cinnamon

### TOPPING

½ cup safflower oil
½ cup brown sugar

½ cup nonroasted coarsely
  chopped nuts

### DOUGH

3¼ cups all-purpose flour
2 tablespoons corn-free baking
  powder
1½ teaspoons salt

¼ cup safflower oil
1½ cups orange juice
2 tablespoons safflower oil

In 9x13–inch pan, mix oil, brown sugar, and nuts; spread evenly. Set aside this topping mixture.

In medium bowl, with fork, mix 3¼ cups flour, baking powder, and salt. With pastry blender or 2 knives used scissor fashion, cut in ¼ cup safflower oil until mixture resembles coarse crumbs; add juice. With fork, quickly mix just until mixture leaves side of bowl (dough will be sticky).

Turn dough onto well-floured surface; knead 6 to 8 strokes, to mix thoroughly. With floured rolling pin, lightly roll dough into a 20x14–inch rectangle. Brush dough with oil.

Sprinkle filling ingredients evenly over dough. Starting with 20-inch side, roll jelly-roll fashion. With sharp knife, cut roll into 16 slices; place over topping, cut side down.

Bake 20 minutes at 400°F or until lightly browned. Invert rolls immediately onto warm platter.

*Makes 16 servings.*

## □ *FRUIT KUCHEN*

### CAKE

| | | |
|---|---|---|
| 1 can (30-ounce) fruit cocktail or other canned fruit packed in its own juice, drained, reserving ¾ cup juice | ½ cup sugar | **Free of:** |
| | ¾ cup safflower oil | Corn |
| | 1 tablespoon corn-free baking powder | Milk |
| | | Soy |
| ⅝ cup potato-starch flour | ¾ teaspoon salt | Wheat |
| 1 1/3 cups ground rolled oats | 1 egg | Yeast |

### TOPPING

| | |
|---|---|
| ½ cup sugar | 1 teaspoon cinnamon |
| 2 tablespoons potato-starch flour | ¼ cup safflower oil |

Set aside drained fruit cocktail. In large bowl, combine all cake ingredients; add the reserved juice, and beat with an electric mixer at low speed until well mixed. Spread batter in greased 9x13x2–inch pan. Evenly spoon fruit over batter. Mix topping ingredients together and crumble topping evenly over fruit.

Bake at 400°F for 30 to 35 minutes or until a toothpick comes out clean. Serve warm or cold.

## □ JAM-DANDY COFFEE CAKE

**Free of:** ⅝ cup potato-starch flour
Corn      2/3 cup ground rolled oats
Milk      ¼ cup sugar
Soy      2½ teaspoons corn-free baking
Wheat       powder
Yeast

¼ cup safflower oil
¾ cup water
1 egg

### TOPPING

2/3 cup jam, any flavor (must be free of corn sweetener or syrup)

¼ cup brown sugar
¼ cup nonroasted chopped nuts

Combine all coffee-cake ingredients in a medium-size mixing bowl. Beat well for 3 minutes. Pour into a greased 9x9–inch pan.

Spoon jam over top in small "dots"; then sprinkle with brown sugar and nuts.

Bake at 375°F for 25 to 30 minutes.

## □ OATMEAL COFFEE CAKE

**Free of:** 1½ cups boiling water
Corn      1 cup raw rolled oats
Milk      ½ cup safflower oil
Soy      1 cup white sugar
Wheat      1 cup packed brown sugar
Yeast      1 teaspoon pure vanilla extract
     2 eggs

2/3 cup ground rolled oats
⅝ cup potato-starch flour
1 teaspoon corn-free baking soda
½ teaspoon salt
¾ teaspoon cinnamon
¼ teaspoon nutmeg

### TOPPING

*In small bowl combine:*

¼ cup safflower oil

½ cup packed brown sugar

3 tablespoons water

½ cup chopped nuts

¾ cup coconut

In small bowl, pour water over oats; set aside and let stand for 20 minutes.

In large bowl, cream oil and beat in the sugars. Blend in vanilla and eggs. Stir in oats. Add sifted flour, soda, salt, and spices; mix well. Pour batter into a greased 9x13–inch or a 12x15–inch pan.

Bake at 350°F for 50 to 55 minutes or until a toothpick comes out clean. Do *not* remove from pan.

Spread topping over baked cake. Broil cake in oven about 6 inches below top of the oven for 1 minute or until bubbly. Take care not to burn the top.

## □ RHUBARB COFFEE CAKE

¼ pound butter (1 stick)

1 egg

2 cups unsifted pure wheat pastry flour

1½ cups brown sugar

1 teaspoon baking soda

2 scant cups raw (well-washed) rhubarb, chopped

**Free of:**

Corn

Soy

Yeast

### TOPPING

½ cup chopped nuts

1 tablespoon sugar

1 teaspoon cinnamon

In medium-size mixing bowl, cream together dough ingredients. Dough will be thick and stiff. Pat into a greased 9x13x2–inch pan. Mix topping and sprinkle over dough.

Bake at 350°F for 35 minutes.

## □ *SOUR CREAM COFFEE CAKE*

**Free of:**
Corn
Soy
Yeast

1 stick butter (¼ pound)
1 cup white sugar
2 eggs
2 cups pure wheat pastry
    flour

1½ teaspoons corn-free baking
    powder
½ teaspoon baking soda
1 cup sour cream
1 teaspoon pure vanilla extract

### TOPPING

½ cup brown sugar
½ cup white sugar
2 teaspoons cinnamon

5 tablespoons crisp rice cereal,
    crushed
4 tablespoons melted butter

Mix topping ingredients together thoroughly and set aside.

Cream butter and sugar together in large mixing bowl; add eggs one at a time, beating well after each. In separate bowl, sift together dry ingredients and add to egg mixture alternately with sour cream and vanilla. Mix well. Batter will be a little stiff. Spread half the batter in greased 9x13–inch or 12x15–inch pan. Cover with half of topping, remaining batter, and rest of topping.

Bake at 350°F for 35 minutes.

## □ *WHEATLESS DOUGHNUTS*

**Free of:**
Milk
Wheat
Yeast

2 2/3 cups ground rolled oats
1 1/3 cups potato-starch flour
1 cup white sugar (divided)
3¼ teaspoons corn-free baking
    powder
1 teaspoon salt
¾ cup brown sugar, packed

2/3 cup safflower oil
3 eggs, beaten
3 tablespoons Rich's
    Coffee-Rich nondairy creamer
2 teaspoons pure vanilla extract
½ teaspoon cinnamon

In large mixing bowl, combine 1/3 cup white sugar, baking powder, salt, brown sugar, flour, and oats. Make a hole in center of dry ingredients and add nearly all of the oil, retaining a little, eggs, creamer, and vanilla. Stir just until dry ingredients are moistened.

Turn onto lightly floured board; roll ½-inch thick. Cut with a 2¾-inch floured doughnut cutter. Place doughnuts on greased baking sheet, 1 inch apart. Cover and refrigerate 1½ hours or overnight.

Mix cinnamon and remaining 2/3 cup white sugar; set aside.

Bake doughnuts at 400°F until done, 10 to 12 minutes. Remove from baking sheet. Brush with remaining oil and roll in cinnamon-sugar mixture.

*Makes 24 to 27 doughnuts.*

## □ *BAVARIAN RYE BREAD*

*1 package active dry yeast*
*1 heaping tablespoon salt*
*1½ cups warm water (100°–115°F, approximately) or enough to make a heavy, pastelike dough*

*3¾ cups rye flour*
*safflower oil*

**Free of:**
Corn
Egg
Milk
Soy
Wheat

Combine the yeast, salt, and water in a mixing bowl. Add the flour, cup by cup, stirring with a wooden spoon to incorporate as much of it as you can.

Turn out on a floured board and knead enough to blend the ingredients. You will have a very heavy dough with little or no life, so shape it as best you can into a ball and place in a small oiled bowl, turning to coat the surface with oil. Cover the bowl with plastic wrap to seal, and then cover with foil. Let rest in a semiwarm area for 16 to 18 hours.

Uncover. You will note that little or nothing has happened to the dough. Punch it down anyway and knead it on a board lightly floured with rye flour for a minute or two. (You'll find it easier to handle than the original mass.) Oil an 8x4x2–inch loaf tin and shape the dough to fit it. Cover and let rise in a warm, draft-free spot until doubled in bulk.

Bake in a preheated 375°F oven, 45 to 50 minutes, or until the bread sounds hollow when tapped on top and bottom. The finished loaf will be about 2½ inches high.

*Makes 1 loaf.*

## □ EGG CASSEROLE BREAD

**Free of:**
Corn
Milk
Soy

5½–6½ cups unsifted all-purpose flour
2 tablespoons sugar
1 tablespoon salt
2 packages active dry yeast

2 tablespoons safflower oil
2 cups very warm tap water (120°–130°F)
3 eggs (at room temperature)

In a large bowl, thoroughly mix 1½ cups flour, sugar, salt, and undissolved dry yeast. Add oil. Gradually add very warm water to dry ingredients and beat 2 minutes at medium speed of electric mixer, scraping bowl occasionally. Add eggs and ½ cup flour. Beat at high speed 2 minutes, scraping bowl occasionally. Stir in enough additional flour to make a soft dough. Cover; let rise in warm place, free from draft, until doubled in bulk, about 35 minutes. Stir down; turn into 2 greased 1½-quart casseroles. Cover; let rise in warm place, free from draft, until doubled in bulk, about 40 minutes.

Bake at 375°F about 35 minutes, or until done. Remove from casseroles and cool on wire racks.

*Makes 2 loaves.*

## □ EGG-FREE BREAD

| | | |
|---|---|---|
| 1 package active dry yeast | 3 tablespoons safflower oil | **Free of:** |
| 2¼ cups warm water | 2 tablespoons molasses | Corn |
| 1 teaspoon sugar | 1½ teaspoons salt | Egg |
| 3½ cups wheat flour | 2 cups whole-wheat flour | Milk |
| | | Soy |

In large bowl, dissolve yeast in water; add sugar and 2½ cups wheat flour. Mix well and let rise until bubbly, about 20 minutes. Add oil, molasses, salt, and whole-wheat flour; beat well. Knead in just enough of the remaining 1 cup wheat flour to make a soft dough. Knead dough until it is smooth and elastic. Let rise in a lightly oiled bowl until dough doubles. Punch down; divide in two and roll out each piece to fit into 2 lightly greased 8¼x4½–inch loaf pans. Allow to rise again.

Bake in a 375°F oven for 40 minutes, or until bread sounds hollow when tapped. Turn bread out to cool on a wire rack.

*Makes 2 loaves.*

## □ MILWAUKEE RYE BREAD

| | | |
|---|---|---|
| 1½ cakes yeast | 2 cups sifted all-purpose flour | **Free of:** |
| 2 cups hot potato water | 1 cup riced potatoes, solidly | Corn |
| 1 tablespoon salt | packed | Egg |
| 4 cups rye flour | 1 teaspoon caraway seed | Milk |
| | | Soy |

In large bowl, dissolve yeast in ¼ cup warm potato water; add remaining liquid. Stir in rest of ingredients and mix well. In bowl, knead until dough is smooth and elastic. Cover bowl with plastic wrap; put in warm place until dough is double in bulk. Form into 2 loaves. Let rise until double in bulk; brush tops of loaves with water.

Bake at 375°F for 40 to 50 minutes or until done.

*Makes 2 loaves.*

## □ *WHITE BREAD*

**Free of:**
Corn
Egg
Milk
Soy

7¾–8¾ cups unsifted all-purpose
   flour
3 tablespoons sugar
4½ teaspoons salt
3 packages active dry yeast

1/3 cup safflower oil
2 2/3 cups very warm tap water
   (120°–130°F)
peanut oil

In a large bowl, thoroughly mix 3 cups flour, sugar, salt, and undissolved dry yeast. Add oil. Gradually add tap water to dry ingredients and beat 2 minutes at medium speed of electric mixer, scraping bowl occasionally. Add ½ cup flour. Beat at high speed 2 minutes, scraping bowl occasionally. Stir in enough additional flour to make a stiff dough. Turn out onto lightly floured board; knead until smooth and elastic, about 10 to 12 minutes. Cover with plastic wrap, then a towel. Let rest 20 minutes. Divide dough in half. Roll each half to a 14x9–inch rectangle. Shape into loaves. Place in 2 greased 9x5x3–inch loaf pans. Brush with peanut oil. Cover loosely with plastic wrap. Refrigerate 2 to 12 hours. When ready to bake, remove from refrigerator. Uncover dough carefully. Let stand at room temperature 10 minutes. Puncture any gas bubbles that may have formed with a greased toothpick or metal skewer.

Bake at 400°F 35 to 40 minutes or until done. Remove from baking pans and cool on wire racks.

*Makes 2 loaves.*

# 10

# Recipes for Casseroles/ Noodles/ Stuffings

## ☐ CHEESE BAKE

2 cups uncooked macaroni or
   other small pasta that is
   egg-free and soy-free
½ cup butter
2 tablespoons flour

1½ cups milk
1 teaspoon salt
¼ teaspoon pepper
1 cup grated Romano cheese
paprika

**Free of:**
Corn
Egg
Soy
Yeast

    Prepare macaroni or other small pasta according to general directions on package. Drain in colander. In pot used for cooking pasta, melt butter. Add flour and cook, stirring constantly for 2 minutes. Do not brown. Stir in milk, salt, and pepper. Cook until smooth and thickened. Combine macaroni with white sauce. Pour into a buttered 11x7–inch casserole. Top with cheese. Sprinkle with paprika.

Bake in a 350°F oven for 25 to 30 minutes. Place under broiler for a few minutes if a browner crust is desired.

*Makes 6 servings.*

## ☐ *CORN AND CHEESE CASSEROLE*

**Free of:**
Soy
Wheat
Yeast

3 cups corn kernels, frozen or. canned
½ cup minced onion
½ cup diced green pepper
4 eggs, lightly beaten

¼ teaspoon ground black pepper
1½ cups milk
1 cup shredded Romano cheese
1½ cups RyKrisp crumbs
¾ teaspoon salt

In a large bowl, combine corn with remaining ingredients; mix well. Pour into a buttered 2-quart casserole; cover and bake at 350°F for 30 minutes; uncover and bake for 30 minutes longer or until golden and a knife inserted in center comes out clean.

*Makes 6 servings.*

## ☐ *ITALIAN CASSEROLE*

**Free of:**
Corn
Egg
Soy
Yeast

2 cups uncooked pasta that is egg-free and soy-free
1 cup CREAMED CELERY SOUP (page 269–70)
1 cup milk
1 cup grated Romano cheese

1 tablespoon minced onion
¼ teaspoon black pepper
½ teaspoon parsley
¼ teaspoon oregano
2 cups cooked meat, cut in ½-inch slices

Prepare pasta according to package directions. Drain. Combine soup, milk, and cheese. Simmer, stirring occasionally, until cheese is melted. Mix pasta, cheese sauce, green pepper, onion, and seasonings. Pour into a buttered 1½-quart casserole. Arrange meat on top of casserole.

Bake in a 325°F oven for 30 minutes.

*Variations:* Meat can be cubed and combined with pasta-and-cheese mixture. Substitute one 7½ ounce can of tuna packed in water for the meat.

*Makes 4 to 6 servings.*

## □ MATZO PUDDING

| | | Free of: |
|---|---|---|
| 20 matzo sheets | ¾ cup grape juice or grape wine | Corn |
| 10 eggs | 1 box currants or raisins | Milk |
| 9 apples, peeled and diced | 2 lemons, juice and rind | Soy |
| 1 large jar apricot jam (must be free of corn sweetener and syrup) | 1 orange, juice and rind | |
| | 1 teaspoon cinnamon | |
| | 1 cup sugar | |
| 1 jar plum jam (must be free of corn sweetener and syrup) | 1 teaspoon salt | |

Pour boiling water over matzos. Drain well. Mix all ingredients together. Put in greased pans, 9x13 inches or larger.

Bake at 325°F for 1½ to 2 hours; better if baked longer.

Matzo Pudding may accompany an entrée or be served as a main course with salad and fruit.

(Above recipe may be cut in half.)

*Makes 2 to 3 9x13x2-inch baking pans.*

## □ TUNA CASSEROLE #1

**Free of:**

Corn
Soy
Wheat
Yeast

1 can (13-ounce) water-packed
    tuna, drained and flaked
1½ cups CREAMED CELERY
    SOUP (pages 269–70)
2/3 cup uncooked rolled oats

½ cup chopped onion
½ cup chopped celery
2 eggs
1 tablespoon lemon juice
ready-to-eat crisp rice cereal,
    crumbled

Preheat oven to 350°F. Grease an 8x4–inch loaf pan. In a large bowl, combine all ingredients except rice cereal and stir until well mixed. Spoon into loaf pan; top with rice cereal.

Bake 45 minutes or until loaf is lightly browned and begins to pull away from sides of pan.

*Makes 6 servings.*

## □ TUNA CASSEROLE #2

**Free of:**

Corn
Egg
Soy
Wheat
Yeast

½ cup chopped onion
1 can (6½-ounce) water-packed
    tuna, drained
1 cup celery, thinly sliced

¼ teaspoon onion powder
½ cup frozen peas
1½ cups CREAMED CELERY
    SOUP (pages 269–70)

Combine ¼ cup onions with other ingredients. Place in greased casserole. Bake at 350°F for 25 minutes. Sprinkle remaining onions on top. Bake 5 minutes longer.

*Makes 4 or 5 servings.*

## □ TUNA-ALMOND CASSEROLE

¾ cup whole blanched almonds
¼ cup safflower oil
½ cup chopped onion

½ cup chopped green pepper
3 cups cooked rice
1 can (8-ounce) water-packed
   tuna, drained

**Free of:**
Corn
Egg
Milk
Soy
Wheat
Yeast

Chop ½ cup almonds; place oil in skillet. Add onion, green pepper, and chopped almonds; sauté slightly. Combine with rice and tuna. Put in casserole dish with rest of almonds on top.
Bake 15 minutes at 425°F.

*Makes 6 servings.*

## □ TUNA-CHEESE CASSEROLE

1 package (8-ounce) shell pasta,
   egg-free and soy-free
2 cups CREAMED CELERY SOUP
   (pages 269-70)
2 slices processed American
   cheese

¼ teaspoon pepper
1 can (7-ounce) water-packed
   tuna, drained
paprika

**Free of:**
Corn
Egg
Soy
Yeast

Cook shells as package directs. In a greased 2-quart casserole, combine soup, American cheese, and pepper. Bake at 350°F for 5 minutes or until cheese is bubbly. Remove from oven and add tuna and shells; mix thoroughly. Sprinkle outer edge with paprika. Return casserole to oven and bake at 350°F for 30 minutes.

## □ *CURRIED RICE WITH CHICKEN LIVERS*

**Free of:**
Corn
Egg
Milk
Soy
Wheat
Yeast

1½  cups uncooked rice
2½ cups pure beef broth
1-2 teaspoons curry powder
1 teaspoon onion powder
8 ounces chicken livers

2 tablespoons safflower oil
½-1 teaspoon salt
paprika
SEASONING MIX (page 156)

Prepare rice according to package directions, using 2½ cups pure beef broth as liquid, adding curry powder and onion powder. Meanwhile, in frying pan, sauté chicken livers in oil over moderate heat until tender. Sprinkle lightly with SEASONING MIX and paprika. Add cooked livers and any rich pan juices to cooked rice. Toss lightly until well mixed and serve at once.

*Makes 4 to 5 servings.*

## □ *RICE WITH CHICKEN CASSEROLE*

**Free of:**
Corn
Egg
Milk
Soy
Wheat
Yeast

2 tablespoons safflower oil
2 cups pure quick-cooking rice
2 cups pure chicken broth

4 tablespoons freeze-dried chives
1 cup cooked chicken, finely
  diced

Put oil in saucepan; add rice and cook over low heat, stirring frequently until rice is golden brown. Add all other ingredients; bring to boil, and simmer about 5 minutes. Remove from heat, place in chafing dish, cover and keep warm for 15 minutes. Fluff gently with fork before serving.

*Makes 4 servings.*

# □ SALMON-VEGETABLE CASSEROLE

2 tablespoons chopped onion
1 tablespoon butter
1½ cups CREAMED CELERY
    SOUP (pages 269–70)
¼ cup milk
½ cup mild Romano cheese,
    shredded

2 cups cooked potatoes, diced
1 cup cut green beans, cooked
1 tablespoon diced pimiento
1 can (7¾-ounce) salmon, drained
2 tablespoons crisp rice cereal
    tossed with melted butter

**Free of:**
Corn
Egg
Soy
Wheat
Yeast

In large saucepan, cook onion in butter until tender. Blend in soup, milk, and cheese. Heat until cheese melts; stir often. Add potatoes, green beans, and pimiento. Pour 1/3 of the mixture into a 1-quart casserole.

With 2 forks, break salmon into chunks; place half of salmon on top of potato mixture. Repeat layers. Top with remaining potato mixture; sprinkle rice cereal on top.

Bake at 400°F for 20 minutes.

*Makes 4 servings.*

# □ KUGEL #1 (NOODLE PUDDING)

3 eggs, separated
1 pound medium egg noodles,
    cooked according to package
    directions

salt to taste
½ pint (1 cup) sour cream
1 pound creamed cottage cheese
¼ pound butter, melted

**Free of:**
Corn
Soy
Yeast

In small bowl, beat egg whites until stiff; set aside. In large bowl, beat yolks until light. To yolks, add remaining ingredients; stir well. Fold in egg whites. Pour into 9x13–inch greased pan and dot top with butter.

Bake at 350°F for 60 minutes.

## □ *KUGEL #2 (NOODLE PUDDING)*

| Free of: | 1 pound egg noodles | 2 tablespoons cinnamon |
|---|---|---|
| Corn | 4 eggs | 1 cup orange juice |
| Milk | 1 teaspoon salt | 4 tablespoons safflower oil |
| Soy | 1 cup sugar | |
| Yeast | 2 cups sliced pie apples or pitted cherries | |

Cook noodles as package directs; drain. In cooking pot, combine cooked noodles, eggs, salt, and sugar; mix very thoroughly. Add sliced pie apples or pitted cherries, cinnamon, and orange juice; mix well. Pour into greased 9x13x2-inch baking pan. Brush top with safflower oil. Bake at 350°F for 45 minutes.

## □ *BEEF OR POULTRY STUFFING*

| Free of: | 24 RyKrisps | 2 tablespoons finely cut onion |
|---|---|---|
| Corn | ¾ cup pure beef or chicken broth | ¼ teaspoon salt* |
| Egg | ¼ cup safflower oil | ⅛ teaspoon pepper |
| Milk | ¼ cup finely cut celery | 2 tablespoons finely cut green pepper |
| Soy | 2 tablespoons finely cut parsley | |
| Wheat | | |
| Yeast | | |

Break RyKrisps into small pieces. Soak in hot stock. Add remaining ingredients. Mix well. Stuff cavity of whole bird, planning on approximately 1 cup per pound of bird. To serve accompanying poultry, place stuffing in greased casserole and bake at 325°F for 30 minutes or until brown.

*Makes 3 cups.*

*Omit when using Seasoned RyKrisps.

## □ POTATO KUGEL

| | | |
|---|---|---|
| 4 large potatoes, peeled and cubed | ⅛ teaspoon pepper | **Free of:** |
| 2 eggs | 1 small onion (optional) | Corn |
| 1 teaspoon salt | ¼ cup potato starch | Milk |
| ¼ teaspoon corn-free baking powder | 2 tablespoons safflower oil | Soy |
| | | Wheat |
| | | Yeast |

In blender, combine all ingredients *except* potato starch and oil. Blend until lumps are gone. Add starch. Blend until thoroughly mixed.

Pour oil into 9x9x2-inch baking pan and coat pan thoroughly; some oil will be left in the bottom of the pan. Pour batter into the pan and spoon remaining oil over top.

Bake 25 to 30 minutes at 400°F or until top of pudding is golden.

## □ POULTRY STUFFING

| | | |
|---|---|---|
| 16 ounces matzo | ¼ cup safflower oil | **Free of:** |
| 1 large onion | ¼ teaspoon salt | Corn |
| 3 medium carrots | ⅛ teaspoon pepper | Milk |
| 2 large sprigs parsley | ⅛ teaspoon garlic powder | Soy |
| 2 eggs | 1-2 tablespoons onion powder | Yeast |

Put matzo, onion, carrots, and parsley through food grinder or processor. Put matzo mixture in large bowl and add beaten eggs, oil, and seasonings.

Stuff fowl with mixture. If there is too much stuffing for the cavity, bake in greased casserole dish for 30 minutes at 350°F.

*Makes enough for a large bird.*

## □ *RICE STUFFING*

**Free of:**

Corn
Egg
Milk
Soy
Wheat
Yeast

¼ cup chopped onion
½ cup chopped celery
2 tablespoons safflower oil
2 cups cooked rice, white
   or wild

¼ teaspoon sage
¼ teaspoon thyme
½ teaspoon salt

In large frying pan, sauté onion and celery in oil until they are transparent. Add rice and seasonings. Mix thoroughly and stuff the fowl or bake separately in a casserole at 350°F for 45 minutes.

*Makes enough for a 4-pound fowl.*

# Recipes for Cereals

## □ CEREAL-NUT MIX

½ cup brown sugar
½ cup dark corn syrup
1/3 cup safflower oil
½ teaspoon salt
6 cups puffed rice or Rice Chex

1 cup nonroasted pecan halves,
   walnuts, or peanuts,
½ cup slivered almonds,
   nonroasted

**Free of:**
Egg
Milk
Soy
Wheat
Yeast

Heat sugar, syrup, oil, and salt in 3-quart pot until sugar dissolves. Stir in mix of cereal and nuts. Bake at 325°F in 9x13-inch pan for 15 minutes. Loosen after 10 minutes. Cool 1 hour. Store in airtight container.

*Makes 7 to 8 cups mix.*

## □ CINNAMON OATMEAL

**Free of:**
Corn
Egg
Milk
Soy
Wheat

3 cups water
¼ teaspoon salt
1 tablespoon cinnamon

¼ cup raisins (or more)
1½ cups rolled oats

Combine ingredients in a 2-quart saucepan. Bring mixture to a boil and cook 1 minute. Reduce heat to simmer and cover; cook about 5 minutes or until cereal is thick. Serve with honey to taste.

*Makes 3 portions.*

## □ FAMILIA

**Free of:**
Corn
Egg
Milk
Soy

2 2/3 cups rolled oats
2 2/3 cups rolled wheat
2 cups raw wheat germ
¾ cup ground nuts
1 cup sunflower seeds

1 cup raisins
1 cup dried fruit, chopped
(Familia is traditionally made
with apples)

Stir all of the ingredients together in a large mixing bowl, then store in a covered container. Serve with milk, yogurt, buttermilk, honey, or maple syrup; however, *serve Familia without milk when following a milk-free diet.*

*Makes approximately 10 to 12 cups.*

# □ *GRANOLA*

| | | |
|---|---|---|
| 2 cups rolled oats | 1/3 cup dried, shredded coconut | **Free of:** |
| ¼ cup rice bran | 1/3 cup honey | Corn |
| ½ cup sunflower seeds | 1 teaspoon vanilla | Egg |
| ½ cup sesame seeds | ¼ teaspoon salt | Milk |
| ¼ cup rice flakes | ½ cup safflower oil | Soy |
| 1 teaspoon cinnamon | ½ cup chopped nuts, nonroasted | Wheat |
| 1/3 cup dried, shredded coconut | | Yeast |

Combine ingredients in a 9x13x2-inch baking pan. Bake at 350°F for 10 minutes; stir thoroughly, scraping the pan. Continue baking until golden in color, about 10 to 15 minutes. Remove from oven. Stir thoroughly. Allow to cool; then store in airtight container. If lumpy, break apart gently with a fork.

*Makes approximately 6 cups.*

# Recipes for Cheese/ Eggs

## ☐ BLINTZES

### PANCAKE

3 eggs
1 1/3 cups water

1 cup flour
¼ teaspoon salt

**Free of:**
Corn
Soy
Yeast

### FILLING

1 pound dry cottage cheese
2 eggs
½ teaspoon pure vanilla extract

1 teaspoon sugar (optional)
½ teaspoon cinnamon
   (optional)

For pancake, in medium bowl, beat eggs; add half of
the water, then the flour, salt, and remaining water. Beat

with electric mixer or with whisk until smooth. Let rest while mixing the filling.

To make the filling, in small bowl, combine cheese, eggs, and seasonings and beat until smooth; set aside.

Lightly grease a 6-, 7-, or 8-inch skillet and heat on top of stove. Pour just enough pancake batter in pan to coat thinly, tilting it from side to side and pouring out excess. Fry only on one side and turn out, brown side up, on a towel. Repeat until batter is used up, adding a little more water if it thickens.

Place 1 heaping teaspoon of filling on each pancake and fold envelope-style. Refrigerate or freeze until ready to fry or bake. Sauté in safflower oil until brown on both sides or bake in a greased pan in a 375°F oven for 35 minutes or until brown. Serve with sour cream and hot BLUEBERRY SAUCE (page 262), or strawberry sauce, or with preserves that do not contain corn syrup or corn sugar. Or serve with sour cream and caviar and omit sugar and cinnamon.

Note: If frozen, thaw in refrigerator before browning.

Makes 22 to 24 blintzes.

## □ CHEESE-PANCAKE SANDWICH

Free of:     PANCAKE
Corn
Soy
Yeast

¼ pound butter
4 teaspoons sugar
3 large eggs

2 cups pure wheat pastry
  flour
1½ teaspoons baking powder
1¼ cups milk

**FILLING**

| | |
|---|---|
| 1½ pounds creamed cottage cheese | 1 teaspoon salt |
| | 2 eggs |
| 3 tablespoons melted butter | |

To prepare pancake, cream butter and sugar; add eggs. Add flour and baking powder alternately with milk and mix well. Place half of the batter (about 1½ cups) into a well-greased 13x9–inch baking dish.

To prepare filling, beat together cottage cheese, butter, salt, and eggs. Spoon filling over batter and top with remaining batter.

Bake in a 350°F oven 45 minutes, until golden brown. Cut into squares and serve hot with sour cream or honey.

*Makes 6 to 8 servings.*


## □ *CHEESE QUICHE*

| | | |
|---|---|---|
| 1 pie shell, partially baked in 9-inch pie pan (see PASTRY, FRENCH-STYLE, page 188) | ½ cup sour cream | **Free of:** |
| | 1 cup milk | Corn |
| | ¼ teaspoon salt | Soy |
| 1 tablespoon dried chives | dash nutmeg | Yeast |
| 1½ cups grated Romano cheese | dash pepper | |
| 3 eggs, well beaten | | |

Sprinkle chives over bottom of crust, grated cheese over chives. Beat together eggs, sour cream, milk, and seasonings. Pour over cheese.

Bake on lowest shelf in oven, on cookie sheet, at 400°F for 30 minutes. Let set for 10 minutes before cutting.

## □ *CHEESE SOUFFLÉ*

*Free of:*
Corn
Soy
Yeast

1 cup milk
4 teaspoons butter
2½ tablespoons pure wheat
   pastry flour
4 egg yolks
½ teaspoon salt

⅛ teaspoon white pepper
5 egg whites, at room
   temperature
½ cup grated Romano cheese
pinch of salt
⅛ teaspoon cream of tartar

Preheat oven to 400°F. Put milk in a saucepan on low heat. Put butter in another large saucepan. Melt butter and add flour, stirring constantly. Cook the flour and butter for 3 minutes. Do not brown. Take the flour-butter mixture off the heat and pour in the boiling milk, all at once, stirring with a wire whisk. Put the pan back on the heat and allow to come to a boil, stirring constantly. Boil for 1 minute. Add the 4 egg yolks, 1 at a time, stirring each in thoroughly with a wire whisk. Add the salt and white pepper. Stop!

You can make this much of a soufflé ahead of time if you are having guests. Cover the saucepan; reheat the mixture to lukewarm before adding the beaten egg whites. Or you can go right ahead and finish the soufflé; it will be ready 20 to 25 minutes later.

Add the cheese to the sauce and stir well. Put the egg whites in a large mixing bowl. Add a pinch of salt and the cream of tartar. Beat whites until stiff. Add ¼ of the egg whites to the cheese sauce and stir them in. Add the remaining ¾ egg whites to the cheese sauce and very carefully fold them in, being sure not to overmix. Pour the mixture into an 8-inch soufflé dish. Place it in the center of the oven. Bake the soufflé 20 to 25 minutes and serve immediately.

**Variation:** Add 1 tablespoon minced onion to the butter and cook slightly before adding the flour.

*Makes 4 to 6 servings.*

## □ *CHEESE TOASTY SANDWICH*

| | | |
|---|---|---|
| 1 egg | chicken, turkey, ham, sliced | **Free of:** |
| ¼ cup milk | Romano cheese, sliced | Corn |
| 4 slices NO-YEAST DOUGH | butter | Soy |
| BREAD (page 116) | | Yeast |

Beat egg lightly; add milk; stir. Dip—do not soak—the sandwiches, filled with meat and cheese, into the mixture, turning to coat both sides. Sauté in butter on both sides, using a skillet or electric frying pan until golden brown. Serve with fresh fruit.

*Makes 2 sandwiches.*

## □ *EGG-FOO-YUNG*

| | | |
|---|---|---|
| 4 eggs | 2 tablespoons soy sauce | **Free of:** |
| 1½ teaspoons salt | ¾ cup safflower oil | Corn |
| ¼ teaspoon pepper | 1 tablespoon potato starch | Milk |
| ¾ cup chopped onion | 1½ cups pure chicken or | Wheat |
| 1 cup cooked meat (chicken, | beef broth | Yeast |
| beef, pork, shrimp) | 2 tablespoons molasses | |
| 1 cup bean sprouts | | |

Lightly beat eggs, salt, and pepper. Stir in onions, meat, sprouts, and 1 tablespoon soy sauce.

Heat oil in frying pan. Using ¼-cup measure, drop mixture as for pancakes into pan. Fry on both sides until browned. Remove to serving platter.

Mix potato starch to a smooth paste with a little broth. Combine in saucepan with remaining broth, molasses, and remaining soy sauce. Cook over low heat, stirring steadily until thickened. Pour over "omelettes" and serve.

*Makes 4 to 5 servings.*

## □ EGGS BENEDICT

**Free of:**
Corn
Milk
Soy
Wheat
Yeast

3 slices Canadian bacon          ¾ cup CREAM SAUCE (page
4 eggs, poached                        263)

Broil the Canadian bacon and cut each slice in 4 equal pieces. Put 3 of the pieces of Canadian bacon in a sauce dish. Poach the eggs, leaving the yolk soft, and put 1 egg in each dish. Spoon the CREAM SAUCE equally on top of each egg. Garnish with a sprig of parsley.

A bread product may be served beneath the Eggs Benedict only if the individual is not sensitive to the ingredients in the bread product.

*Makes 2 servings.*

**Free of:**
Corn
Soy
Wheat
Yeast

## □ HOT DEVILED EGGS

12 eggs, hard-boiled                    1 teaspoon dry mustard powder
2 cups CREAM SAUCE (page 263)    ¼ cup Romano cheese, grated

Cut the eggs in half lengthwise. Remove yolks and rub them through a sieve. Arrange the egg whites in a shallow glass baking dish. Add the mustard powder and sieved egg yolks to ½ cup of the CREAM SAUCE. Mix well and fill the 24 egg-white halves equally with the mixture.

Pour the remaining 1½ cups of CREAM SAUCE over the tops of the eggs. Sprinkle evenly with the Romano cheese. Bake at 425°F for 15 minutes or until the eggs are lightly browned.

*Makes 4 to 6 servings.*

## □ *OMELETTES*

| 2 eggs | dash pepper | **Free of:** |
|---|---|---|
| 1 tablespoon water | ½ teaspoon safflower oil | Corn |
| dash salt | | Milk |
| | | Soy |
| | | Wheat |
| | | Yeast |

Beat eggs with a fork until frothy. Add 1 tablespoon water, salt, and pepper, and beat again. Meanwhile, melt butter in omelette pan (or 10-inch, cured iron skillet with slanted sides) until sizzling hot.

Turn flame down and pour in beaten egg. The egg immediately starts to set. Using a fork, scrape the set edges of the egg toward the center, tilting the pan at the same time, so that the liquid egg then seeps underneath to cook. When bottom is cooked (the top still runny), fold over 1/3 of the omelette toward the center. Rest the edge of the pan on the plate and quickly turn the pan upside down, so omelette slides out on plate, folded in thirds.

*Variations:* You can make many different types of omelettes. Have whatever you are going to put in the omelette ready when you put the eggs in the pan. Then, before folding the omelette, put the other ingredients on top of the eggs and fold them into the center. Try filling omelettes with seafood, vegetables, fruit, or create a new variety with bits of leftovers.

## ▢ *TOMATO QUICHE*

**Free of:**
Corn
Soy
Yeast

1 9-inch pie crust (PASTRY, FRENCH-STYLE, page 188)
2 tomatoes—ripe, not soft*
1 egg white, slightly beaten
3 eggs
3 cups heavy cream

2 tablespoons butter
1¼ teaspoons salt
¼ teaspoon pepper
½ cup plus 1 tablespoon grated Romano cheese

Prepare pie crust according to directions. Use only ¾ of the pastry; freeze rest for later use. On lightly floured surface, or between two sheets of waxed paper, roll pastry to form 13-inch circle. Use to line bottom and side of 9-inch springform pan. Pastry should measure 2 inches high on side of pan. Pat pastry to fit into pan snugly and evenly.

Preheat oven to 375°F. Scald tomatoes in boiling water 5 to 10 minutes. With sharp knife, pull off skin; remove seeds. Chop pulp coarsely.

Brush bottom of pastry shell very lightly with some of egg white. In medium bowl, combine 3 eggs, cream, butter, salt, and pepper. Beat just until thoroughly combined. Stir in ½ cup cheese.

Drain tomatoes very well on paper towels; layer in pie shell. Pour cheese filling into shell. Sprinkle surface with 1 tablespoon cheese. Bake 55 minutes or until golden brown.

To serve: Cool 5 to 10 minutes. With sharp knife,

*Or use 1 can (14½-ounce) salad-style tomatoes, very well drained.

loosen edge of pastry from side of pan; remove side from springform pan. Serve quiche warm, from bottom of pan placed on serving plate.

*Makes 10 servings.*

# Recipes for Condiments/ Seasonings/ Toppings

## ☐ CRISPY CINNAMON TOPPING

1¼ cups rolled oats, uncooked
1/3 cup firmly packed brown
   sugar
¼ cup safflower oil

1/3 cup nonroasted, chopped
   nuts, if desired
¼ teaspoon cinnamon

**Free of:**
Corn
Egg
Milk
Soy
Wheat
Yeast

Combine all ingredients; mix well. Cook in 10-inch skillet over medium heat, stirring constantly, 5 to 7 minutes or until golden brown. Spread onto ungreased cookie sheet to cool; store in tightly covered container in refrigerator up to 3 months.

Serve as topping over fruit salad, fruit, yogurt, frozen yogurt, ice cream, or pudding.

*Makes about 2 cups.*

## □ *CRISPY HERB TOPPING*

**Free of:**
Corn
Egg
Soy
Wheat
Yeast

2 cups rolled oats, uncooked
1/3 cup safflower oil
1/3 cup grated Romano
   cheese

1/3 cup nonroasted chopped
   nuts, if desired
¼ teaspoon onion or garlic salt

Combine all ingredients; mix well. Bake in ungreased 15½x10½–inch jelly-roll pan in preheated, moderate oven, 350°F, 15 to 18 minutes or until light golden brown. Cool; store in tightly covered container in refrigerator up to 3 months.

Sprinkle over tossed green salads, soups, casseroles, or vegetables.

**Variation:** Add 1 teaspoon oregano leaves and ½ teaspoon thyme leaves to mixture before baking.

*Makes about 3 cups.*

## □ *CRISPY PEANUT TOPPING*

**Free of:**
Corn
Egg
Soy
Wheat
Yeast

¼ cup safflower oil
1/3 cup chunky natural
   peanut butter

2½ cups rolled oats, uncooked
1/3 cup firmly packed brown
   sugar

Melt together oil and peanut butter in medium-size saucepan over low heat, stirring occasionally. Add oats and brown sugar; mix well.

Bake in 15½x10½–inch jelly-roll pan in preheated, moderate oven, 350°F, 15 to 18 minutes or until golden brown, stirring occasionally. Cool. Store in tightly covered container in refrigerator up to 3 months.

Serve as topping over fruit salads, fruits, yogurt, frozen yogurt, ice cream, or pudding.

*Makes about 4 cups.*

## □ KETCHUP

| | | **Free of:** |
|---|---|---|
| 4 cups tomato juice | 2 buds garlic, whole | Corn |
| ¼ cup lemon juice | 1 tablespoon sugar | Egg |

Put tomato juice, lemon juice, and garlic in a saucepan and bring to a boil. Reduce heat to very low and simmer uncovered for about 2½ hours until desired thickness. Remove garlic buds and stir in sugar. Simmer 5 minutes. Store in refrigerator.

Free of:
Corn
Egg
Milk
Soy
Wheat
Yeast

*Makes 1 to 2 cups ketchup.*

## □ SEAFOOD COCKTAIL SAUCE

| | | **Free of:** |
|---|---|---|
| 1 cup KETCHUP (See previous recipe.) | 1 teaspoon horseradish (or more) | Corn |
| 1 tablespoon lemon juice | | Egg |

Free of:
Corn
Egg
Milk
Soy
Wheat
Yeast

Mix together all ingredients and chill. Serve with cold, cooked seafood.

## □ SEASONING MIX

**Free of:**
Corn
Egg
Milk
Soy
Wheat
Yeast

1 tablespoon whole cumin seed
4 inches stick cinnamon
5 whole cloves
1 teaspoon cardamom seed
   (with pods removed)

1 teaspoon whole black peppercorns
2 bay leaves

Combine in blender; cover and blend until ground. When ground, pour into bowl and add:

¼ cup dried parsley leaves
2 tablespoons onion powder
2 tablespoons ground tumeric
4 teaspoons ground coriander

1 teaspoon ground ginger
1 teaspoon garlic powder
1 tablespoon paprika

Stir well to combine. Store in airtight container at room temperature.

*Makes approximately 2 cups mix.*

## □ TOMATO CATSUP

**Free of:**
Corn
Egg
Milk
Soy
Wheat
Yeast

4 quarts peeled, cored, chopped
   ripe tomatoes
1 cup chopped onions
½ cup chopped sweet red peppers
1½ teaspoons celery seeds
1 teaspoon mustard seed

1 teaspoon allspice
1 stick cinnamon
1 cup sugar
1½ cups lemon juice
1 tablespoon paprika

Cook tomatoes, onions, and peppers until soft. Press through a food mill or sieve. Cook rapidly until thick (volume is reduced about one half), about 1 hour. Tie whole spices in a cheesecloth bag; add it with sugar and salt to tomato mixture. Cook gently about 25 minutes, stirring frequently. Add lemon juice and paprika, cook until thick. As mixture thickens, stir frequently to prevent sticking.

Pour, boiling hot, into hot jars, leaving ¼-inch head space. Adjust caps. Process 10 minutes in boiling water bath.

This recipe may be frozen in pint freezer containers.

*Makes about 3 pints.*

# 14

# *Recipes*
# *for*
# *Desserts*

## ☐ *APPLE BUNDT CAKE*

3 cups unsifted all-purpose flour
2 cups sugar
1 teaspoon baking soda
pinch salt
1 teaspoon cinnamon
3 eggs

1¼ cups butter
½ cup milk
3 large apples, peeled and diced
½ cup raisins
½-1 cup chopped nuts,
   nonroasted

**Free of:**
Corn
Soy

### *GLAZE*

1 cup corn-free confectioners'
  or powdered sugar

2 tablespoons lemon juice

Mix dry ingredients. Add wet ingredients. Mix well.
Add apples, raisins, and nuts. Use a greased Bundt pan

and bake at 350°F for 1¼ hours. Remove the pan after 30 minutes and glaze when absolutely cool.


## ◻ *BANANA-OAT CAKE*    *Good*

**Free of:**
Corn
Milk
Soy
Wheat
Yeast

2 cups oat flour
2 teaspoons corn-free baking
    powder
1/3 teaspoon salt
2 eggs

2 tablespoons safflower oil
½ cup light-brown sugar
3 tablespoons water
½ cup mashed bananas

Sift and measure flour. Add baking powder and salt; mix well. Beat eggs and oil together; add sugar and then add water. Alternately add dry mixture and mashed bananas.

Pour into a greased square 8-inch pan. Bake in a 350°F oven for 25 to 30 minutes. Cool in pan and cut into squares.

*Makes 16 pieces.*


## ◻ *CHEESECAKE #1*

**Free of:**
Corn
Egg
Soy
Wheat
Yeast

1 envelope unflavored gelatin
½ cup sugar
1 cup boiling water
2 packages (8 ounces each)
    cream cheese, softened

1 teaspoon pure vanilla extract
    (optional)
1 9-inch OAT PIE CRUST
    (pages 187–88)

In large bowl, mix unflavored gelatin and sugar; add boiling water and stir until gelatin is completely dissolved.

With electric mixer, beat in cream cheese and vanilla until smooth. Pour into prepared crust; chill until firm, about 2 hours. Top, if desired, with fresh or canned fruit.

*Makes about 8 servings.*

## □ *CHEESECAKE #2*

### *CRUST*

1½ cups quick-cooking rolled oats, uncooked

½ cup finely chopped non-roasted chopped nuts

½ cup firmly packed brown sugar

1/3 cup butter

**Free of:**
Corn
Soy
Wheat
Yeast

### *FILLING*

2 packages (8 ounces each) cream cheese, softened

½ cup granulated sugar

1 tablespoon lemon juice

3 eggs

1 cup dairy sour cream or sour half-and-half

### *TOPPING*

1 cup dairy sour cream or sour half-and-half

2 tablespoons granulated sugar

1 to 2 teaspoons pure vanilla extract

For crust, combine all ingredients; mix well. Firmly press into bottom and sides of ungreased 9-inch spring-form pan, about 1½ inches high. Bake in preheated oven, 350°F, about 18 minutes or until golden brown; cool.

For filling, combine cream cheese, sugar, and lemon

juice, mixing at medium speed in electric mixer until well blended. Add eggs, one at a time, beating well after each addition. Blend in sour cream. Pour into prepared crust. Bake in preheated, moderate oven, 350°F, about 50 minutes.

For topping, combine all ingredients; mix well. Spread over baked cheesecake. Continue baking in moderate oven, 350°F, about 10 minutes. Loosen cake from rim of pan; cool before removing rim. Chill several hours before serving. Garnish with fruit, if desired.

*Makes 1 9-inch cheesecake.*

## □ *CHOCOLATE CAKE*

**Free of**:
Corn
Egg
Milk
Soy
Yeast

1½ cups pure wheat pastry
   flour
1 cup sugar
3 tablespoons unsweetened
   cocoa powder
1 teaspoon baking soda

1 teaspoon corn-free baking
   powder
1 teaspoon salt
5 tablespoons safflower oil
1 teaspoon pure vanilla extract
1 cup warm water
1 teaspoon lemon juice

In an ungreased 8x8x2-inch baking pan, combine and mix flour, sugar, cocoa powder, baking soda, baking powder, and salt. Make three holes in mixture. Pour oil into one hole, vanilla into second, and lemon juice into third. Add warm water and mix until blended.

Bake at 350°F for 35 to 40 minutes.

*Makes one 8x8-inch cake.*

# □ DOUBLE-LAYER CAKE

| | | |
|---|---|---|
| 2½ cups sifted pure wheat cake flour | ½ cup safflower oil | **Free of:** |
| | 2 teaspoons powdered egg replacer, packed | Corn |
| 1½ cups sugar | | Egg |
| 3 teaspoons corn-free baking powder | 4 tablespoons water | Milk |
| | 1 cup water | Soy |
| 1 teaspoon salt | 1 teaspoon pure vanilla extract | Yeast |

Sift flour, sugar, baking powder, and salt together. Drop oil into flour mixture. Stir egg replacer and 4 tablespoons water together until smooth. Add ¾ cup water, vanilla, and egg-replacer mixture. Beat 3 or 4 minutes. Add remaining water and beat 3 minutes. Pour into 8-inch cake pans.

Bake in preheated oven at 375°F for 30 to 35 minutes.

*Makes two 8x8-inch layer cakes.*

# □ MANDARIN-ORANGE CAKE

| | | |
|---|---|---|
| 2 cups unsifted pure wheat pastry flour | 2 cans (11 ounces each) mandarin oranges, packed in water (do not drain) | **Free of:** |
| | | Corn |
| 2 cups sugar | | Milk |
| 2 teaspoons baking soda | ¼ teaspoon cinnamon | Soy |
| 2 eggs | ⅛ teaspoon ground cloves | Yeast |
| pinch salt | ⅛ teaspoon allspice | |
| rind of 1 orange, grated | | |

Mix ingredients with spoon only until moistened. Pour into ungreased 9x13x2-inch baking pan. Bake at 350°F for 35 to 45 minutes or until a toothpick comes out clean.

## □ *SPONGE CAKE #1*

Free of:
Corn
Milk
Soy
Wheat
Yeast

4 eggs, separated
2/3 cup sugar
¼ teaspoon salt

2 tablespoons lemon juice
rind of ½ lemon, grated
1 cup rice flour

Beat egg yolks until thick and lemon-colored. Add sugar and salt and beat well. Add lemon juice and grated lemon rind. Gradually add rice flour and beat until smooth.

Let batter stand for about 10 minutes. Then beat egg whites until stiff peaks form. Fold beaten whites into the batter.

Pour into an ungreased 9-inch tube pan and bake in a preheated 350°F oven for 30 minutes, or until top is browned and firm. Invert immediately after removing from oven. Cool completely and remove from pan.

*Makes 12 servings.*

## □ *SPONGE CAKE #2*

Free of:
Corn
Milk
Soy
Wheat
Yeast

4 eggs, separated
1 cup sugar
¼ cup orange juice

1 cup ground millet flour
2 teaspoons corn-free baking
    powder

Beat egg yolks until lemon-colored. Add sugar and beat well. Stir in orange juice. Add millet flour and baking powder, mixing well.

In small mixing bowl, beat egg whites until stiff peaks form. Fold egg whites into batter carefully until completely blended but spongy with air bubbles.

Pour into an ungreased 9-inch tube pan and bake in a preheated 350°F oven for 30 minutes, or until top is browned and firm to the touch. Immediately upon removing from oven, invert tube pan onto a cake rack or onto the neck of an empty soda bottle. Allow cake to cool completely in this upside-down position before removing from pan.

*Makes 10 to 12 servings.*

## □ *CAROB FUDGE*

| | | |
|---|---|---|
| ½ cup toasted carob powder | ¾ cup natural peanut butter | **Free of:** |
| ½ cup dry milk powder | ¾ cup honey | Corn |
| | | Egg |

Combine ingredients in medium bowl. Cut with a fork; then knead the dough until all ingredients are blended. Press dough into 9x9–inch baking pan and refrigerate 2 hours. Cut into 1-inch squares to serve.

Soy
Wheat
Yeast

*Makes 18 pieces.*

## □ *CHOCOLATE CLUSTERS*

| | | |
|---|---|---|
| 6 ounces (1 cup) Nestlé's semi-sweet real chocolate morsels | 1½ cups crisp, ready-to-eat rice, oat, or corn cereal | **Free of:** |
| | 1½ cup salted peanuts | Egg |
| 3 tablespoons corn syrup | | Milk |
| 1 tablespoon water | | Wheat |
| | | Yeast |

In large skillet, combine chocolate morsels, corn syrup, and water; stir over "simmer" or lowest heat until morsels are melted, stirring so the chocolate will not stick to the pan.

Remove from heat when mixture is smooth. Stir in cereal and peanuts. Drop by rounded teaspoonfuls onto waxed paper. Chill until firm.

*Makes 2 to 3 dozen clusters.*

## □ *NATURAL CANDY*

**Free of:**
Corn
Egg
Milk
Soy
Wheat

½ cup pitted dates
½ cup raisins
¼ cup roasted carob powder

⅛ teaspoon salt
½ cup walnuts
½ cup sunflower seeds

Mix dates and raisins with carob and salt; mix in nuts and seeds. Grind mixture in meat grinder. Press together into 1-inch balls. Store in airtight container.

*Makes approximately 24 candies.*

## □ *PEANUT BUTTER CLUSTERS*

**Free of:**
Corn
Egg
Soy
Wheat
Yeast

2 cups sugar
¼ cup cocoa powder
½ cup milk
¼ pound butter

1 teaspoon pure vanilla extract
pinch salt
½ cup natural peanut butter
3 cups quick-cooking rolled oats

In saucepan, combine sugar, cocoa powder, milk, and butter. Put on medium heat and cook mixture until it starts to boil.

Remove saucepan from heat and cool 1 minute. Add vanilla, salt, peanut butter, and rolled oats, and mix well.

Drop by teaspoonfuls on waxed paper. When set, cookies are ready to eat.

*Makes approximately 3 dozen clusters.*

## □ *PEANUT BUTTER CUPS*

1½ cups GRANOLA (page 141)     1 cup peanut butter
1 cup dry milk powder    ½ cup honey

**Free of:**
Corn
Egg
Soy
Wheat
Yeast

In medium bowl, combine ingredients and knead. Place paper liners in muffin cups and press mixture into cups. Refrigerate until firm.

*Makes 8 to 12 cups.*

## □ *PEANUT BUTTER GEMS*

1 cup natural peanut butter    1 teaspoon pure vanilla extract
¼ cup sifted corn-free con-    1 cup mixed dried fruit, chopped
   fectioners' or powdered sugar    2 cups puffed-rice cereal
1/3 cup honey

**Free of:**
Corn
Egg
Milk
Soy
Wheat

Blend together peanut butter, sugar, honey, and vanilla. Stir in mixed fruit and cereal. Roll into small balls. Chill on cookie sheet. Store in covered container in cool place.

*Makes about 50 1½–inch balls.*

## □ *PEANUT-SUGAR MOUNDS*

**Free of:**
Corn
Egg
Milk
Soy
Yeast

½ cup sugar
¾ cup safflower oil
2 cups sifted pure wheat
   pastry flour

2 teaspoons pure vanilla extract
1¾ cups dry-roasted, salted
   peanuts, chopped
sugar

Add sugar gradually to oil, creaming well; blend in flour, vanilla, and peanuts. Shape into 1-inch balls; place on ungreased cookie sheet.

Bake at 350°F for 20 minutes. Roll in sugar while still very warm.

*Makes about 7½ dozen cookies.*

## □ *APPLESAUCE COOKIES*

**Free of:**
Corn
Egg
Milk
Soy
Wheat

1 cup brown sugar
¾ cup safflower oil
1 cup APPLESAUCE (page 208)
½ cup nonroasted nuts,
   chopped

½ teaspoon salt
1 teaspoon pure vanilla extract
4 cups rolled oats
½ cup chopped dates or raisins

Beat brown sugar and oil together until well blended. Add remaining ingredients and mix well. Drop by teaspoonfuls onto baking sheet.

Bake at 375°F for 25 minutes or until well browned. Cool on cookie sheet.

*Makes 5 dozen cookies.*

## □ *CHOCOLATE-PEANUT BUTTER COOKIES*

2 squares (1 ounce each)
   unsweetened baking chocolate
½ cup crunchy natural peanut
   butter
2/3 cup sugar

2 tablespoons safflower oil
1 cup rolled oats, uncooked
¾ cup raisins
½ cup nonroasted nuts,
   chopped

**Free of:**
Corn
Egg
Milk
Soy
Wheat

Melt together chocolate, crunchy peanut butter, and oil in medium-size saucepan over low heat, stirring occasionally until well blended. Stir in remaining ingredients. Drop by rounded teaspoonfuls onto wax paper; chill until firm. Store in refrigerator.

*Makes about 2 dozen no-bake cookies.*

## □ *COOKIES FOR BREAKFAST*

¾ cups potato flour
2/3 cup butter, softened
1/3 cup firmly packed brown
   sugar
1 egg
1 teaspoon pure vanilla extract
½ teaspoon cinnamon

½ teaspoon corn-free baking
   powder
½ teaspoon salt
1½ cups rolled oats, uncooked
1 cup (4 ounces) shredded
   Cheddar cheese
¾ cup raisins
1 cup chopped apple

**Free of:**
Corn
Soy
Wheat

Combine flour, butter, sugar, egg, vanilla, cinnamon, baking powder, and salt in large bowl; mix well. Add oats, cheese, and raisins; mix well. Stir in apple. Drop by heaping tablespoonfuls onto ungreased cookie sheet. Bake in preheated, moderate oven, 375°F, for 15 minutes or until golden brown. Store in tightly covered container in refrigerator or in loosely covered container at room temperature.

*Makes about 2 dozen cookies.*

## □ CRISPY COOKIES

**Free of:**
Eggs
Milk
Soy
Wheat
Yeast

1 package (10-ounce) regular marshmallows (about 40)

3 tablespoons safflower oil
5 cups crispy rice cereal

In large saucepan over low heat, melt marshmallows with oil; stir until completely melted. Cook 3 minutes longer, stirring constantly. Remove from heat. Add cereal and stir until well coated. Using buttered spoon, quickly spread evenly into a greased 9x13x2–inch baking pan. Cool. Cut into 2x2–inch squares.

## □ GRANOLA COOKIES

**Free of:**
Corn
Egg
Milk
Soy
Yeast

1 egg, beaten
1/3 cup safflower oil
1/3 cup honey
½ teaspoon pure vanilla extract

1 cup whole-wheat pastry flour
½ teaspoon salt
½ teaspoon baking soda
1¼ cups GRANOLA (page 141)

Mix egg, oil, honey, and vanilla. Add flour, salt, and soda. Add GRANOLA and mix thoroughly. Place dough by spoonfuls on greased cookie sheet, pressing lightly.

Bake at 325°F for 10 minutes or until slightly brown around the edges.

*Makes 12 large cookies.*

**Free of:**
Eggs
Soy
Wheat
Yeast

## □ MACAROONS

2 2/3 cups flaked, dried coconut
2/3 cup sweetened, condensed milk

1 teaspoon pure vanilla extract

Combine coconut, milk, and vanilla in small mixing bowl. Drop by teaspoonfuls, 1 inch apart, onto well greased baking sheets. Bake at 350°F for 8 to 10 minutes or until lightly browned. Remove at once from baking sheets.

*Note:* This recipe may be doubled.

*Makes 30 cookies.*

## □ *MERINGUE KISSES*

| | | |
|---|---|---|
| 2 egg whites (at room temperature) | 6 ounces Nestlé's semisweet chocolate morsels | **Free of:** Milk |
| ¾ cup sugar | | Wheat |
| | | Yeast |

In a small mixing bowl, with electric mixer, beat egg whites until they are stiff and hold peaks. Fold in sugar and beat. Fold in chocolate chips. Drop by spoonfuls on a greased cookie sheet.

Heat oven to 375°F. When cookies are put into oven, turn off oven. Leave cookies in oven for 3 hours and do *not* open the door before the 3 hours are up. Meringue is "dried" rather than baked. Store in tightly covered container up to 2 weeks.

*Makes 2 to 3 dozen cookies.*

## □ *MOLASSES COOKIES*

| | | |
|---|---|---|
| | | **Free of:** |
| 1/3 cup safflower oil | ½ teaspoon baking soda | Corn |
| 1 cup brown sugar | ½ teaspoon cinnamon | Egg |
| ½ cup molasses | 1 ounce roasted carob powder | Milk |
| 2 cups sifted pure wheat pastry flour | | Soy |
| | | Yeast |

Cream oil, brown sugar, and molasses until thoroughly blended; beat until fluffy. Add flour, baking soda, cinnamon, and carob powder; mix well. Chill dough in refrigerator for several hours. Roll half of the dough out at a time on a lightly floured board until it is ⅛-inch thick. Cut with a cookie cutter.

Bake on a greased cookie sheet at 350°F for 12 to 15 minutes. Cool. These cookies may be frosted and decorated.

*Makes approximately 3 dozen cookies.*

## □ *NO-BAKE COOKIES*

**Free of:**
Corn
Egg
Soy
Wheat
Yeast

2 cups sugar
¼ cup cocoa powder
½ cup milk
¼ pound butter
1 teaspoon pure vanilla extract

pinch salt
½ cup natural chunky peanut butter
3 cups quick-cooking rolled oats

In saucepan, combine sugar, cocoa powder, milk, and butter. Put on medium heat and cook mixture until it starts to boil, stirring to avoid burning. Remove saucepan from heat and cool 1 minute.

Add vanilla, salt, peanut butter, and rolled oats; mix well. Drop by teaspoonfuls onto waxed paper. When set, cookies are ready to eat. Refrigeration may be necessary.

*Makes 2 to 3 dozen cookies.*

## □ *NO-BAKE CRUNCHIES*

½ cup PEANUT BUTTER          ½ cup finely chopped,          **Free of:**
  CRUNCHY SPREAD (page 93)   nonroasted nuts          Corn
½ cup shredded or flaked                          Egg
  coconut                                Milk
                                                  Soy

Combine PEANUT BUTTER CRUNCHY SPREAD and  Wheat
coconut; shape to form ¾-inch balls. Roll in nuts; chill.  Yeast
Store in covered container in refrigerator.

*Makes about 1 dozen no-bake cookies.*

## □ *OATMEAL COOKIES*

1 cup unsifted pure wheat pastry  ¼ teaspoon salt          **Free of:**
  flour                    ¾ cup safflower oil          Corn
1 cup sugar               ½ teaspoon pure vanilla extract  Egg
1 teaspoon baking soda          2 cups rolled oats          Milk
                                                  Soy
                                                  Yeast

In medium bowl, mix flour, sugar, soda, salt, and oil.
When well blended, add vanilla and oatmeal. Shape into
1-inch round balls. Put on a cookie sheet 2 inches apart.
Flatten with the bottom of a glass.

Bake at 350°F for 15 minutes or until golden. Remove
the cookies from the cookie sheet, taking care not to
crack them. Cool cookies on flat surface. Store in airtight
container.

*Makes approximately 3 dozen cookies.*

## □ PEANUT BUTTER REFRIGERATOR COOKIES #1

**Free of:**
Corn
Milk
Soy

2 egg whites, lightly beaten
1 teaspoon pure vanilla extract
1/3 cup date sugar

1 cup natural peanut butter
2 tablespoons sifted all-purpose flour

Combine egg whites, vanilla, and date sugar. Mix well and allow to stand for 10 minutes. Combine egg-white mixture, peanut butter, and flour; mix thoroughly, using a pastry blender or fork. Form the dough into a ball and wrap tightly in waxed paper or foil; refrigerate at least 2 hours.

Divide the cold dough into walnut-size balls and place them evenly on 2 cookie sheets. Press each cookie flat using the tines of a fork.

Bake in a preheated oven at 350°F for 10 to 12 minutes. Be careful in handling them, as they will break easily.

*Makes about 2 dozen cookies.*

## □ PEANUT BUTTER REFRIGERATOR COOKIES #2

**Free of:**
Corn
Milk
Soy
Wheat
Yeast

¾ cup safflower oil
1 cup natural peanut butter
½ cup granulated sugar
1 cup firmly packed brown
    sugar
2 eggs

1 teaspoon pure vanilla extract
2¼ cups ground oat flour
2 teaspoons baking soda
¼ teaspoon salt
1 cup nonroasted chopped
    peanuts

Beat together oil, peanut butter, and sugars; blend in eggs and vanilla. Add combined dry ingredients; mix well. Stir in nuts; chill dough about 1 hour.

Shape to form 1-inch balls. Place on ungreased cookie sheet; flatten with fork dipped in sugar to form crisscross pattern.

Bake in preheated, moderate oven, 350°F, about 10 minutes or until edges are golden brown.

*Makes about 4½ dozen cookies.*

## □ SPICE COOKIES

| | | Free of: |
|---|---|---|
| ½ cup safflower oil | ¾ teaspoon salt | |
| ½ cup packed brown sugar | ¾ teaspoon cinnamon | Egg |
| ¼ cup corn syrup | ½ teaspoon ginger | Milk |
| ¼ cup honey | ¼ teaspoon ground cloves | Soy |
| 3¼ cups sifted pure wheat pastry flour | | Yeast |

With electric mixer, cream oil and sugar; blend in corn syrup and honey. Add the dry ingredients and blend well.

Shape dough into two rolls 2 inches in diameter; wrap and refrigerate. Dough may be kept in the refrigerator up to 2 weeks. When ready to use, slice dough ⅛-inch thick. Place on a greased cookie sheet.

Bake at 350°F for 12 to 15 minutes. Cool on rack.

*Makes about 4 dozen cookies.*

## □ APPLE BARS

| | | Free of: |
|---|---|---|
| | | Corn |
| 2 cups sifted pure wheat pastry flour | 3 full cups thinly sliced apples, peeled | Egg |
| 1 teaspoon salt | ½ teaspoon cinnamon | Milk |
| 1 cup sugar | ¼ teaspoon nutmeg | Soy |
| 1/3 cup safflower oil | | Yeast |

Combine flour, salt, and sugar; cut in oil with a fork until dough is crumbly. Remove ¾ cup and set aside.

Press remaining mixture into an 8x8x2-inch greased cake pan. Bake at 350°F for 15 minutes.

Remove from oven and spread evenly with apple slices. Sprinkle with cinnamon and nutmeg. Sprinkle with the reserved crumbs, evenly covering the apples.

Bake at 350°F for 30 to 35 minutes. Cool. Slice into 1x2-inch bars.

*Makes 32 bars.*

## □ APRICOT BARS

**Free of:**
Corn
Egg
Milk
Soy
Wheat

### FILLING

1½ cups (½ pound) dried apricots
1 cinnamon stick (2 inches)
4 whole cloves

¾ cup brown sugar, firmly packed

### CRUMB MIXTURE

½ cup safflower oil
1 cup brown sugar

1 box RyKrisp, crushed to 2 2/3 cups

To prepare filling, put apricots and spices in medium-size saucepan. Add water just to cover apricots and spices. Cover and simmer until tender. Drain. Remove spices. Mash apricots. Mix thoroughly. Cool.

To prepare crumb mixture, preheat oven to 400°F. Butter a pan 9x13x2 inches. Cream oil and sugar. Add RyKrisp crumbs and mix thoroughly. Press half of mixture to cover bottom of pan. Spread with filling. Pat remaining crumb mixture on top.

Bake 15 to 20 minutes or until lightly browned. Cut into 30 bars. Cool and remove from pan.

*Makes 30 bars.*

## □ BROWNIES

| | | Free of: |
|---|---|---|
| 1 cup sugar | ½ teaspoon corn-free baking | **Free of:** |
| 2 eggs | powder | Corn |
| ¼ cup safflower oil | ¼ teaspoon salt | Milk |
| ½ cup cocoa powder | ½ cup chopped nonroasted | Soy |
| 1 teaspoon vanilla | nuts | Yeast |
| 2/3 cup pure wheat pastry | | |
| flour | | |

In bowl, combine sugar, eggs, oil, cocoa powder, and vanilla. Beat until creamy. Add flour, baking powder, and salt; mix well. Add nuts and mix. Spread in greased 8x8x2-inch baking pan.

Bake at 350°F for 25 to 30 minutes. Cool and cut into 2-inch squares.

*Makes 16 squares.*

## □ BROWNIES FOR BREAKFAST

| | | **Free of:** |
|---|---|---|
| 1 cup brown sugar | ¼ cup dry cocoa powder | **Free of:** |
| ½ cup broken, nonroasted | ½ teaspoon corn-free baking | Corn |
| walnuts | powder | Soy |
| 1 cup wheat germ | 2 eggs | Yeast |
| ⅛ teaspoon salt | ½ cup safflower or sunflower oil | |
| 2/3 cup dry milk powder | 1 tablespoon molasses | |

In mixing bowl, combine dry ingredients. Add slightly beaten eggs, oil, and molasses. Mix well. Stir into well-greased 8x8–inch baking pan.

Bake at 350°F for 30 minutes. Turn out of pan while hot. Cut into 4 equal portions. Serve.

## ☐ *CHOCOLATE-PEANUT BUTTER BARS*

**Free of:**
Corn
Soy
Wheat
Yeast

1 cup natural peanut butter
½ cup sugar*
1 egg

1 package (4 ounces) Baker's German sweet chocolate (broken in pieces)

Mix peanut butter, sugar, and egg until blended. Press into 10x7–inch rectangle on ungreased baking sheet.

Bake at 325°F for 20 minutes. Remove from oven.

*Immediately* arrange chocolate on top of dough and cover lightly with aluminum foil. Let stand for 3 minutes. Remove oil and spread chocolate over entire surface. *Immediately* cut into 2x1–inch bars. Cool.

*Makes about 30 bars.*

*Use 1 cup sugar for sweeter bar.

## ☐ *DATE BARS*

**Free of:**
Corn
Milk
Soy
Wheat

safflower oil
3 eggs
2/3 cup brown sugar, firmly packed
10 RyKrisps, crushed to 1 cup

1¼ cups (7 ounces) finely chopped dates
¾ cup nonroasted nuts, chopped

Preheat oven to 325°F. Grease a square 8- or 9-inch pan with oil. In medium bowl, beat eggs until thick and foamy. Add brown sugar gradually. Beat in RyKrisp crumbs, dates, and nuts. Mix thoroughly. Pour into pan.

Bake 35 to 40 minutes or until firm to the touch. Loosen sides with knife. Let stand 15 minutes before cutting.

*Makes 15 bars (1½ x 2 inches).*

## □ GRANOLA-PEANUT BUTTER BARS

| | | |
|---|---|---|
| ½ cup light corn syrup | 3 cups GRANOLA (page 141) | **Free of:** |
| 2/3 cup natural peanut butter | | Egg |
| | | Milk |

Grease 9x9x2-inch pan. In 3-quart saucepan, heat corn syrup to boiling; boil just 1 minute and remove from heat. Stir in peanut butter. Stir in GRANOLA and mix until smooth. Pat mixture into pan with dampened spoon. Cool in refrigerator 1 hour. Cut into bars.

Free of: Soy Wheat Yeast

*Makes 18 one-inch bars.*

## □ LEMON BARS

### CRUST

| | | |
|---|---|---|
| ¼ pound butter | ¼ cup corn-free powdered | **Free of:** |
| 1 cup sifted pure wheat pastry | sugar or 2 1/3 tablespoons | Corn |
| flour | granulated sugar | Soy |
| | | Yeast |

## FILLING

2 eggs

1 cup granulated sugar

2 tablespoons pure wheat pastry
  flour

3 tablespoons lemon juice

½ teaspoon corn-free baking
  powder

¼ teaspoon salt

Mix crust ingredients. Press into 9x9x2–inch pan. Bake at 350°F for 20 minutes.

Meanwhile, beat filling ingredients until smooth. Pour over hot crust.

Bake at 350°F for 30 minutes. Cool. Sprinkle with powdered sugar and cut into 1-inch squares.

*Makes 18 squares.*

## □ MARSHMALLOW CRISPS

**Free of:**
Egg
Milk
Wheat
Yeast

12 RyKrisps (1 cellophane pack)   ¼ cup flake coconut, firmly
½ cup marshmallow cream           packed

Preheat oven to 350°F. Spread RyKrisp with marsh-mallow cream. Sprinkle with coconut. Bake 8 minutes or until lightly browned.

*Note:* Nuts may be substituted for coconut.

*Makes 12 crisps.*

## □ OATMEAL BARS

**Free of:**
Corn
Egg
Wheat
Yeast

4 cups rolled oats, uncooked
1 cup butter
1 cup brown sugar
½ cup sugar

1 cup Baker's semisweet
  chocolate morsels
1 cup natural peanut butter

Mix together all ingredients except chocolate chips and peanut butter and pat into 10x15-inch jelly-roll pan.

Bake in preheated 350°F oven 12 minutes.

Warm chocolate morsels and peanut butter together in small saucepan over low heat. Watch carefully to avoid burning. Frost with this mixture and cut into bars before completely cooled.

*Makes 75 two-inch bars.*

## □ *PEANUT BUTTER NUTTY BARS*

### DOUGH

| | | |
|---|---|---|
| 1/3 cup safflower oil | 1¼ cups sifted pure wheat pastry | **Free of:** |
| ½ cup firmly packed brown | | Corn |
| sugar | | Egg |
| | | Yeast |

### TOPPING

| | |
|---|---|
| 6 ounces Nestlé's semisweet chocolate chips | 2/3 cup natural peanut butter (chunky or smooth) |

In 9x13x2-inch pan, put oil. Add brown sugar and mix with a fork. Add flour, and mix with fork until ingredients are thoroughly combined. Pat into bottom of pan to form crust. Bake at 350°F for 10 minutes, *not more.*

In saucepan, melt chocolate chips with peanut butter. Spread this mixture over baked crust. Refrigerate 30 minutes or until chocolate layer is firm, *not hard.* Cut into squares. Store in refrigerator.

*Makes approximately 4 dozen bars.*

## □ STRAWBERRY-OATMEAL BARS

**Free of:**
Corn
Egg
Milk
Yeast

1 pouch (15-ounce) Quaker oatmeal-cookie mix
½ cup strawberry preserves
   without corn syrup or
   corn sugar

1/3 cup nonroasted nuts,
   chopped
1 teaspoon lemon juice

Combine all ingredients; mix well. Press into a greased 13x9x2–inch pan. Bake in a preheated 375°F oven for 20 minutes. Cool; cut into bars.

*Makes about 4 dozen bars.*

## □ APPLE STRUDEL

### DOUGH

**Free of:**
Corn
Egg
Soy
Yeast

2 cups sifted pure wheat pastry
   flour
½ teaspoon salt
2 tablespoons sugar

3 teaspoons corn-free baking
   powder
7 tablespoons butter
2/3 cup milk

### FILLING

melted butter
4 to 6 medium apples, thinly sliced
1/6 cup sugar

½ teaspoon cinnamon
1/3 cup nonroasted walnuts,
   finely chopped

Into large mixing bowl, put flour, salt, sugar, and baking powder. Cut in butter; add milk. Form into 2 balls. Roll each out on floured board until it is ¼-inch thick.

Spread each rolled-out ball with melted butter, apples, sugar, cinnamon, and walnuts. Roll like a jelly roll, pinch ends together, and place on greased cookie sheet.

Bake at 375°F for 35 to 40 minutes. When cool, slice into ¾-inch slices.

## □ *MOCK STRUDEL*

**FILLING**

| | | |
|---|---|---|
| 1 large jar apricot preserves, without corn syrup or sweetener | 1 cup coconut<br>1 cup nonroasted nuts, chopped | **Free of:**<br>Corn<br>Egg<br>Soy |

**PASTRY**

Yeast

1 cup sour cream
½ pound butter

2 cups unsifted pure wheat pastry flour

Combine filling ingredients in small bowl and set aside.

In medium-size bowl, combine the sour cream, butter, and flour. Use a fork to cut the ingredients together; knead the dough if necessary. Form into a ball; cover the bowl tightly; refrigerate several hours or overnight.

When ready to make, divide dough into 4 equal parts. Roll out one at a time on a floured board. Spread each with ¼ of the filling and roll up jelly-roll fashion. Pinch ends together.

Bake on a cookie sheet at 350°F for 30 minutes or until golden. When cool, slice rolls into ¾-inch slices.

*Makes about 5 dozen pastries.*

## □ *FIVE-MINUTE CUSTARD*

**Free of:**
Corn
Soy
Wheat
Yeast

½ cup dry milk powder
¼ cup sugar
⅛ teaspoon salt

2 cups fresh milk
2 eggs
1 teaspoon pure vanilla extract

Combine milk powder, sugar, and salt in a 2-quart cooking pot and stir well. Add ½ cup fresh milk and two eggs and heat until smooth. Add 1½ cups fresh milk and cook over medium heat for about 4 minutes or until *almost* boiling. Remove from heat and cool to room temperature. Stir in 1 teaspoon vanilla. Serve warm or cold. Good for breakfast, snack, or dessert.

*Makes 4 to 6 ½-cup servings.*

## □ *FRUIT CUSTARD*

**Free of:** 1 8-ounce glass buttermilk          1 cup strawberries, raspberries,
Corn     sugar to taste                                   blueberries, or peaches,
Egg                                                                fresh or frozen, without syrup
Soy
Wheat          Put all ingredients into blender and blend thoroughly.
Yeast     Soft-freeze, reblend, then serve.

## □ *PEANUT CUSTARD*

**Free of:** 1 cup oats (quick or old-          1/3 cup chunk-style natural
Corn          fashioned, uncooked)                peanut butter
Egg       ¾ cup milk                                  ¼ cup honey
Soy       ½ cup nonroasted, unsalted          ¼ teaspoon salt
Wheat          peanuts, chopped                    1 cup half-and-half
Yeast

Combine all ingredients except half-and-half in large bowl; mix well. Cover; refrigerate 4 to 5 hours or overnight.

Mix well; fold in half-and-half. Spoon into dessert dishes; chill.

***Variation:*** Substitute ½ cup nonroasted, unsalted pecans, walnuts, or almonds for peanuts and 3 tablespoons cocoa powder for peanut butter.

*Makes 6 servings.*

## □ *BANANA ICE CREAM*

| | | |
|---|---|---|
| ½ cup orange juice | 1 tablespoon sugar | **Free of:** |
| 3 ripe, firm, medium bananas, | dash salt | Egg |
| cut in chunks | 1 cup whipped Rich's Rich Whip | Milk |
| 12 regular-size marshmallows | | Soy |
| (egg-free) | | Wheat |
| | | Yeast |

Combine all ingredients in blender. Whip until stiff (if possible) and bananas are completely smooth and blended. Pour into 8x8x2-inch baking pan. Cover with foil and freeze until firm. Will keep in freezer up to 2 weeks.

*Makes approximately 6 servings.*

## □ *STRAWBERRY ICE CREAM*

| | | |
|---|---|---|
| 1 envelope unflavored gelatin | 1 10-ounce package frozen | **Free of:** |
| ¾ cup sugar | strawberries, thawed and | Egg |
| 2 cups liquid Rokeach Coffeelite | chopped | Milk |
| (see package directions) | 2 cups Rich's Rich Whip, | Soy |
| | whipped until stiff | Wheat |
| | | Yeast |

In medium saucepan, combine gelatin, sugar, and creamer. Let stand 1 minute. Stir over low heat until gelatin is completely dissolved, about 5 minutes.

Remove from heat; stir in strawberries. Chill, stirring occasionally, until mixture mounds slightly when dropped from spoon. Fold whip into gelatin mixture. Pour into 2 freezer trays (4x10 inches) or an 8-inch baking pan, and freeze until firm.

*Makes about 1½ quarts.*

## □ WATERMELON ICE

**Free of:**
Egg
Milk
Soy
Wheat
Yeast

2 cups watermelon, diced and seeded     1 cup light corn syrup
2 tablespoons lime juice

In medium bowl, mash watermelon until almost smooth. Add corn syrup and lime juice, stirring until well mixed. Pour into a 1-quart freezer container; cover and freeze 2 to 3 hours or until almost firm. Beat with wooden spoon until smooth. Return to freezer until firm.

*Makes about 3 cups.*

## □ PEANUTTY POPS

**Free of:**
Egg
Milk
Wheat
Yeast

1 envelope unflavored gelatin     1 cup natural peanut butter
½ cup sugar     1 cup Rich's Coffee-Rich
1 cup boiling water

In medium bowl, mix gelatin and sugar; add boiling water and stir until gelatin is dissolved. With electric mixer or wire whip, blend in peanut butter and creamer. Pour into 5-ounce paper cups. Freeze until partially firm; then insert sticks and freeze until firm.

*Variation:* Stir in carob chips, chopped banana, or mini-marshmallows just before inserting stick.

*Makes 6 pops.*

## □ *LIME SHERBET*

| | | Free of: |
|---|---|---|
| 1 envelope unflavored gelatin | 4 drops green food coloring | Corn |
| 1 cup sugar | 1 tablespoon grated lime peel | Egg |
| 1½ cups boiling water | 2½ cups Rich's Coffee-Rich | Milk |
| ½ cup lime juice | | Wheat |
| | | Yeast |

In large bowl, mix gelatin with sugar. Add boiling water and stir until gelatin is completely dissolved; add lime juice, coloring, and peel. Cool completely and stir in creamer.

Freeze 1½ hours or until mixture is frozen about ½ inch around the sides of bowl. Beat with electric mixer or wire whip until smooth, about 2 minutes. Pour into 2 freezer trays (4x10 inches) or an 8-inch baking pan, and freeze until firm.

*Makes about 1½ quarts.*

## □ *OAT PIE CRUST*

| | | Free of: |
|---|---|---|
| 1 cup oats, uncooked | 3 tablespoons safflower oil | Corn |
| 1/3 cup nonroasted nuts, finely chopped | ½ teaspoon cinnamon | Egg |
| | | Milk |
| 1/3 cup firmly packed brown sugar | | Soy |
| | | Wheat |
| | | Yeast |

Combine all ingredients; mix well. Press onto bottom and sides of very lightly oiled 9-inch pie plate. Bake in preheated, moderate oven, 375°F, for 8 to 10 minutes or until golden brown. Cool; chill or freeze as filling requires.

*Makes 9-inch pie crust.*


## □ PASTRY, FRENCH-STYLE

**Free of:**
Corn
Soy
Yeast

2 cups sifted pure wheat pastry flour
2 tablespoons sugar
½ teaspoon salt

½ cup butter
1 egg, beaten
2 tablespoons cold water

Sift flour once and measure; add sugar and salt; sift again. Cut in butter using fork. Add egg; stir. Sprinkle in water, mixing lightly.

When moistened, press into a ball; cover with a damp cloth and let stand 10 minutes. Roll very thin on floured board. Place rolled dough in pie dish; trim to fit and pierce bottom with fork.

Bake at 375°F for 10 minutes or until brown.

*Makes 2 9-inch pie shells, or 3 thin shells.*


## □ RYE CRUMB CRUST

**Free of:**
Corn
Egg
Milk
Soy
Wheat
Yeast

15 RyKrisps, crushed to 1 cup
¼ cup sugar

¼ cup safflower oil
2 teaspoons hot water

Butter an 8-inch pie plate. Combine crumbs and sugar. Add oil and water. Blend thoroughly. Press crumbs evenly and firmly onto bottom and sides of pie plate. Form an edge around top of crust, not on rim of plate.

Bake 15 minutes at 400°F. Cool thoroughly. Fill with a fruit or gelatin filling. Refrigerate until time for serving.

*Makes 1 8- or 9-inch pie shell.*

## □ SCHAUM TORTE

| | | Free of: |
|---|---|---|
| 3 *egg whites* | 1 *cup sugar* | Corn |
| ¼ *teaspoon cream of tartar* | | Milk |

Heat oven to 275°F. With electric mixer, beat egg whites and cream of tartar until frothy. Gradually beat in sugar a little at a time. Beat until very stiff and glossy.

Put a sheet of brown paper on baking sheet. Spread egg-white mixture on the brown paper in an 8- or 9-inch circle, heart, or any desired shape. Mound gently with the back of a spoon.

Bake 60 minutes at 275°F. Turn oven off and leave in until cold.

Fill with ice cream topped with fresh berries or cut-up fruit.

Free of: Soy, Wheat, Yeast

## □ AMBROSIA CRISP

Free of:

1 *package (10-ounce) "dry" frozen strawberries, thawed, then sliced*

1 *can (8¼-ounce) pineapple chunks, packed in water or own juice*

6 *tablespoons packed brown sugar*

1 *tablespoon potato starch*

1 *can (11-ounce) mandarin oranges packed in water, drained*

¼ *cup shredded coconut*

¼ *cup quick-cooking rolled oats*

2 *tablespoons oat flour*

⅛ *teaspoon cinnamon*

1 *tablespoon safflower oil*

Corn
Egg
Milk
Soy
Wheat
Yeast

Drain strawberries and pineapple, reserving liquid; combine to make 1 cup. Set aside.

In 10x6x2–inch baking pan, combine 2 tablespoons of the sugar and the potato starch. Slowly blend in the juice. Add fruits and coconut and stir until well coated.

In small bowl, mix remaining sugar, oats, flour, and cinnamon. Cut in oil. Sprinkle evenly over fruits. Bake at 350°F for 30 to 35 minutes or until top is golden.

*Makes 6 servings.*


## □ *APPLE COBBLER #1*

**Free of:** *3–4 pounds apples, thinly sliced*    *1 teaspoon corn-free baking*
Corn    *1 cup rolled oats, uncooked*     *powder*
Milk    *1 cup sugar*       *1 egg*
Soy    *1 teaspoon cinnamon*
Wheat
Yeast

Spread apples in a 9x13x2–inch pan; apples should be about 1½ inches tall. In small bowl, combine the remaining ingredients and pour evenly over apples. Squeeze lemon juice over topping. Bake 45 minutes at 350 °F.


## □ *APPLE COBBLER #2*

**Free of:** *4–6 cups thinly sliced apples*    *2 eggs, beaten*
Corn    *2 cups pure wheat pastry*     *1 teaspoon pure vanilla extract*
Milk      *flour*            *2/3 cup safflower oil*
Soy    *1 cup sugar*          *¾ cup nonroasted walnuts,*
Yeast    *1½ teaspoons baking soda*     *chopped*
      *1 teaspoon salt*

Spread apples over bottom of 9x13x2–inch baking pan. Add dry ingredients and mix. Add remaining ingredients. Stir with fork only until blended. Smooth batter evenly in the pan.

Bake at 350°F for 40 to 50 minutes or until cake springs back when lightly touched. Cool. Serve warm or cold.

## □ *APPLE-RHUBARB COBBLER*

| | | |
|---|---|---|
| 3 cups peeled and sliced Golden Delicious apples | 1 cup brown sugar | **Free of:** |
| | ¾ cup rolled oats | Corn |
| 2 cups diced rhubarb | 1 teaspoon cinnamon | Egg |
| 2 tablespoons lemon juice | ½ teaspoon salt | Milk |
| 1 cup oat flour | 1/3 cup safflower oil | Soy |
| | | Wheat |
| | | Yeast |

Combine apples and rhubarb in 9x13x2–inch baking dish. Sprinkle with lemon juice. Mix dry ingredients together with oil in a small bowl until crumbly. Spoon evenly over fruit.

Bake at 350°F for 45 to 50 minutes or until fruit is soft and top begins to brown.

## □ *TORTONI*

| | | |
|---|---|---|
| 4 cups Rich's Rich Whip | 1 teaspoon pure vanilla extract | **Free of:** |
| ¼ cup toasted almonds, chopped | ⅛ teaspoon nutmeg | Egg |
| | | Milk |
| 1 teaspoon rum extract (optional) | | Soy |
| | | Wheat |
| | | Yeast |

Whip the Rich Whip in a large mixing bowl. Stir in almonds, extracts, and nutmeg. Spoon mixture into 2½-

inch fluted paper or foil liners in muffin tins. Freeze. Serve plain or top each torte with a dollop of whipped cream.

*Makes 8 servings.*

## □ *BLUEBERRY-CHEESE PIE*

**Free of:**
Egg
Soy
Wheat
Yeast

1 package (3-ounce) cream cheese, softened
1 can (14-ounce) Eagle Brand sweetened condensed milk
1/3 cup lemon juice

1 teaspoon pure vanilla extract
1 OAT PIE CRUST (pages 187–88)
BLUEBERRY SAUCE (page 262) or other fruit topping

In medium bowl, beat cream cheese until light and fluffy. Gradually beat in sweetened condensed milk. Stir in lemon juice and vanilla. Pour into pie crust. Chill 2 hours. Top with BLUEBERRY SAUCE or other fruit topping before serving. Refrigerate leftovers.

*Makes one 8- or 9-inch pie.*

## □ *CHOCOLATE AND ICE-CREAM PIE*

**Free of:**
Egg
Soy
Wheat
Yeast

**CRUST**

1 package (4 ounces) Baker's German sweet chocolate

2 tablespoons butter
2 cups dried, flaked coconut

**FILLING**

1 quart any flavor natural ice cream, softened
2 cups whipped cream, already whipped

1 cup dried, flaked coconut

To make crust, melt chocolate in pan over lowest heat, stirring constantly so the chocolate will not stick. Add butter. When melted, remove from heat and stir in coconut. Mix well. Press into bottom and sides of pie plate. Freeze until hard.

Spread ice cream into crust. Spread with whipped topping and sprinkle with coconut. Freeze until firm. Remove from freezer about 10 minutes before serving and dip pan into hot water to soften crust slightly, to ease cutting.

*Makes one 8- or 9-inch pie.*

## □ CUSTARD PIE

| | | Free of: |
|---|---|---|
| 3 cups milk | 1 baked 9-inch OAT PIE CRUST | Corn |
| 1/3 cup powdered egg replacer | (pages 187–88) or RYE CRUMB | Egg |
| ½ cup sugar | CRUST (pages 188–89) | Soy |
| ¼ teaspoon salt | nutmeg | Wheat |
| 1 teaspoon pure vanilla extract | | Yeast |

Scald 2½ cups of the milk. In large bowl, stir egg replacer into ½ cup of unscalded milk until smooth. Add sugar, salt, and vanilla, stirring until smooth. Gradually add hot scalded milk, stirring constantly. Pour into custard cups or baked pie shell. Sprinkle top with nutmeg. Let cool.

*Makes 8- or 9-inch pie or 4 to 6 custard cups.*

## □ LEMON PIE

| | | Free of: |
|---|---|---|
| | | Corn |
| ¼ cup powdered egg replacer | 2 tablespoons lemon rind | Egg |
| 1 cup sugar | 1 baked 9-inch pie shell, OAT PIE | Milk |
| ¼ teaspoon salt | CRUST (pages 187–88) or RYE | Soy |
| 1½ cups hot water | CRUMB CRUST (pages 188–89) | Wheat |
| 1/3 cup lemon juice | | Yeast |

In double boiler, combine egg replacer, sugar, and salt. Stir with rubber spatula until thoroughly blended. Add water, lemon juice, and lemon rind. Continue stirring until smooth and thick. When dropped from spatula, it should mound.

Remove from heat. Stir for 5 minutes to cool. Pour into pie shell. Let cool thoroughly. Refrigerate at least 2 hours before serving.

*Makes 8- or 9-inch pie.*

## □ SCRUMPTIOUS PIE

**Free of:**
Corn
Egg
Soy
Wheat
Yeast

**CRUST**

1 cup raw rolled oats

½ cup nonroasted slivered
   almonds

½ cup brown sugar

1/3 cup safflower oil

**FILLING**

1 cup boiling water

1 small package (3-ounce)
   orange gelatin dessert

1 pint softened natural vanilla
   ice cream

2 cups fresh peaches, sliced

To make crust, toast oats in pie plate at 350°F for 5 minutes. Add almonds and toast 5 minutes more. Add sugar and oil, blend, and press to form a crust in the pie plate. Set aside.

In medium bowl, pour boiling water over gelatin. Stir well. Add ice cream and stir until ice cream is smooth. Fold in peaches. Pour mixture into crust and refrigerate.

*Makes 8- or 9-inch pie.*

# □ *YOGURT PIE #1*

1 envelope plus 1½ teaspoons
  unflavored gelatin (about 4½
  teaspoons)
½ cup water
3 8-ounce cartons (3 cups)
  natural unflavored yogurt
½ cup honey

Dash of salt
1½ cups heavy cream, whipped
OAT PIE CRUST (pages 187–88)
BLUEBERRY SAUCE (page
  262) or other fruit sauce

**Free of:**
Corn
Egg
Soy
Wheat
Yeast

Soften gelatin in water; stir over low heat until dissolved. Combine yogurt, honey, and salt, mixing until well blended. Gradually add dissolved gelatin; mix well.

Chill about 15 minutes or until slightly thickened. Fold in whipped cream. Chill 45 minutes or until mixture mounds when dropped from spoon; mound into OAT PIE CRUST. Chill 4 hours or until firm.

Serve with BLUEBERRY SAUCE or other flavor fruit sauce.

*Makes 9-inch pie.*

# □ *YOGURT PIE #2*

2 cartons (8 ounces each) natural
  unflavored yogurt
1 carton (8-ounce) whipped
  cream

OAT PIE CRUST (pages 187–88)
  or RYE CRUMB CRUST (pages
  188–89)

**Free of:**
Corn
Egg
Soy
Wheat
Yeast

In a large bowl, combine yogurt and whipped cream. Mix well. Pour into crust, mounding slightly. Freeze.

Remove from freezer 10 minutes before serving. Garnish with fresh fruit.

*Makes 6 to 8 servings.*

## □ *CHEESE SNACKERS*

**Free of:**
Corn
Soy
Yeast

¼ teaspoon white pepper
½ teaspoon salt
1 cup soft butter
2 eggs

2 cups (½ pound) shredded
  Romano cheese
2¼ cups pure wheat pastry
  flour

Combine all ingredients except flour in mixing bowl; mix well. Blend in flour. Shape into 2 12-inch rolls. Wrap in foil or waxed paper; refrigerate several hours.

Cut into ⅛-inch slices. Place on ungreased cookie sheets.

Bake at 400°F for 9 to 12 minutes, or until light brown on edges. Serve as is or with dip.

*Makes about 12 dozen.*

## □ *CINNAMON CRISPS*

**Free of:**
Corn
Egg
Milk
Soy
Wheat
Yeast

12 RyKrisps
1–1½ tablespoons safflower oil

2 tablespoons sugar
1 teaspoon cinnamon

Preheat oven to 400°F. Spread crackers lightly with oil. Mix sugar and cinnamon and sprinkle on crackers. Bake 5 minutes. Serve warm or cold.

**Free of:**
Corn
Egg
Milk
Soy
Wheat
Yeast

## □ *FROZEN POPSICLES*

1 package (3 ounces)
  orange-flavored gelatin
½ cup sugar

2 cups boiling water
2 cups fresh orange juice

Dissolve gelatin and sugar in boiling water. Add orange juice. Pour into ice-cube trays, small paper cups, or frozen-popsicle molds. Insert wooden sticks or paper spoons diagonally in each ice-cube section, or at an angle in molds or cups, for handles. Freeze until firm, 2 to 3 hours.

*Makes 20 to 24 popsicles.*

## □ *GELATIN BLOCKS*

3 packages (3 ounces each)
  fruit-flavored gelatin,
  all the same flavor

4 envelopes unflavorea gelatin
4 cups boiling water

**Free of:**
Corn
Egg
Milk
Soy
Wheat
Yeast

Combine ingredients and mix thoroughly in a 9x13x2-inch baking pan until all powders are dissolved. Refrigerate and chill until firm. Cut into 1-inch squares. Store in refrigerator.

*Makes about 48 squares.*

## □ *NUT MIX*

2 cups each of the following dry-roasted nuts, seeds, and fruits:
  roasted almonds, plain
  toasted sunflower seeds
  toasted pumpkin seeds
  roasted peanuts, salted
    or plain

toasted cashews, bits and
  pieces
raisins (more than 2 cups if
  desired)
whatever other nuts and
  seeds are desired

**Free of:**
Corn
Egg
Milk
Soy
Wheat

Combine above ingredients in large bowl and mix. Store in covered container. Serve as snack or hors d'oeuvres. This recipe is yeast-free if raisins are deleted.

# Recipes
## for
## Fish / Seafood

## ☐ BUTTER-HERB BAKED FISH

½ cup butter
2/3 cup crushed ready-to-eat
  rice cereal
¼ cup grated Romano cheese
½ teaspoon each basil leaves,
  oregano leaves, and salt

¼ teaspoon garlic powder
1 pound frozen sole or perch
  fillets, thawed and drained, or
  fresh fish

**Free of:**
Corn
Egg
Soy
Wheat
Yeast

In 13x9–inch pan, melt butter in preheated 350°F oven
(5 to 7 minutes). Meanwhile, in 9-inch pie pan, combine
cereal, Romano cheese, basil, oregano, salt, and garlic
powder. Dip fillets in butter and then in crumb mixture,
and arrange in baking pan.
Bake near center of 350°F oven for 25 to 30 minutes or

until fish is tender and flakes with a fork. Serve immediately.

*Makes 4 servings.*

## □ *FILLET OF SOLE #1*

**Free of:**    1 pound sole or flounder fillets    ¾ cup white wine
Corn    salt    ¼ pound seedless green grapes
Egg    1 tablespoon fresh lime juice    1½ tablespoons safflower oil
Milk    1 teaspoon dried parsley    1 tablespoon potato starch
Soy    ¼ teaspoon tarragon    2 tablespoons fresh orange juice
Wheat    ½ clove garlic, minced

Sprinkle fish fillets lightly with salt and lime juice. Place in lightly greased skillet. Sprinkle with parsley, tarragon, and garlic. Add wine and simmer 12 to 15 minutes until fish flake easily and look milky white, not transparent. Add grapes the last 5 minutes. Remove fillets from heat but keep warm on a separate platter.

In the original skillet, mix oil with remaining juices and blend in potato starch until smooth. Add orange juice and cook, stirring until mixture thickens. Add more wine if desired. Pour sauce over fillets.

*Makes 3 to 4 servings.*

## □ *FILLET OF SOLE #2*

**Free of:**    2 pounds sole or turbot fillets    1½ cups CREAMED CELERY
Corn    2 tablespoons butter, cut into      SOUP (pages 269–70)
Egg      dots    3 tablespoons sherry
Soy    ½ teaspoon salt    3 tablespoons slivered almonds
Wheat    2 packages (10 ounces    1 tablespoon melted butter
     each) frozen chopped spinach,    2 tablespoons grated Parmesan
     cooked and drained      cheese

Wash, drain, and dry the fish fillets. Arrange in a baking dish and dot with 2 tablespoons butter. Sprinkle with salt, cover the dish with foil, and bake in a preheated 350°F oven for 15 minutes. Remove from oven and drain liquid.

Spread cooked spinach over the top of the fish. Blend soup with sherry and pour over all. Mix almonds with melted butter and cheese and sprinkle over top. Bake uncovered for 20 minutes at 350°F.

*Makes 6 to 8 servings.*

## □ FILLET OF SOLE #3

| | | |
|---|---|---|
| 1 pound fresh or frozen fillet | salt | **Free of:** |
| of sole | pepper | Corn |
| safflower oil | paprika | Egg |
| | | Milk |

Defrost fillets (if frozen) and arrange in a shallow baking dish. Brush lightly with oil; sprinkle with seasonings. Bake uncovered at 350°F for 30 to 35 minutes or until fork-tender. Serve with colorful side dishes.

Soy
Wheat
Yeast

*Makes 3 or 4 servings.*

## □ HALIBUT SALAD

**Free of:**
Corn

| | | |
|---|---|---|
| 1 pound halibut, thawed and | 1 onion, sliced | Milk |
| drained | 1 teaspoon salt | Soy |
| 1 carrot | 1 cup SAUCE ADRIENNE | Wheat |
| 1 rib celery | (page 261) | Yeast |

Cook halibut and vegetables in simmering salted water for 15 to 20 minutes. Do not boil. Fish will flake easily with a fork when done.

Drain, cool, and bone. Chill thoroughly. Flake the fish and dress with SAUCE ADRIENNE. Garnish with sliced hard-cooked eggs and serve on lettuce.

## □ SALMON LOAF

**Free of:**
Corn
Soy
Wheat
Yeast

2 cups (16-ounce can) cooked salmon
2 lightly beaten eggs
1 cup low-fat milk
2 tablespoons finely chopped green pepper

1 tablespoon finely chopped onion
2 tablespoons lemon juice
½ teaspoon salt
⅛ teaspoon pepper

Mix all ingredients together and pour into a greased loaf pan. Bake for 35 minutes at 350°F or until knife inserted in center comes out clean.

Serve hot with a green salad or serve cold with a hot vegetable. Also may be used cold as a sandwich spread.

**Variation:** Use tuna instead of salmon.

*Makes 1 loaf.*

## □ SALMON SOUFFLÉ

**Free of:**
Corn
Soy
Wheat
Yeast

1 can (1-pound) salmon, drained and flaked
1/3 cup crisp, ready-to-eat rice cereal, crumbled
¼ cup snipped parsley
salt and pepper to taste
½ cup sour cream
¼ cup BLENDER MAYONNAISE (page 257)

¼ cup milk
1 tablespoon lemon juice
½ teaspoon dry mustard
2 eggs, slightly beaten
paprika
lemon slices

Mix the salmon, crumbled rice cereal, parsley, salt, and pepper in a greased 2-quart casserole. Mix together sour cream, mayonnaise, milk, lemon juice, mustard, and eggs.

Pour over salmon. Sprinkle with paprika and bake in a preheated 350°F oven for 30 minutes. Garnish with lemon slices.

*Makes 4 servings.*

## □ *SHRIMP CURRY*

| | | |
|---|---|---|
| ½ cup finely chopped onion | ¼ teaspoon seasoned pepper | **Free of:** |
| 1½ tablespoons safflower oil | 2 cups pure chicken broth | Corn |
| 2 tablespoons potato starch | 2 cups fresh shrimp, cooked | Egg |
| 1 teaspoon seasoned salt | cooked rice | Milk |
| 1 teaspoon curry powder | | Soy |
| | | Wheat |

Sauté onions in oil for 5 minutes. Blend in potato starch and seasonings. Slowly add broth, stirring constantly. Bring to a boil, reduce heat, and simmer gently about 10 minutes, stirring occasionally. Add shrimp and heat through. Serve over rice.

*Makes 4 to 6 servings.*

## □ *SHRIMP WITH PEA PODS (STIR-FRIED)*

| | | |
|---|---|---|
| 4 tablespoons safflower oil | 2 tablespoons pure chicken | **Free of:** |
| 1 teaspoon fresh ginger, finely chopped | stock | Corn |
| ¾ pound uncooked shrimp, shelled and deveined | 1 tablespoon soy sauce | Egg |
| | salt | Milk |
| ¼ cup sliced bamboo shoots | 1½ teaspoons sugar | Wheat |
| 1 pound fresh or frozen pea pods | cooked rice | |

Heat 2 tablespoons oil in wok or large frying pan. When hot, add ginger and stir-fry 10 seconds. Add shrimp and stir-fry for about 1½ minutes or until shrimp changes color. Add additional 2 tablespoons oil, bamboo shoots, and pea pods; stir-fry 2 minutes. Add chicken stock, soy sauce, salt to taste, and sugar; stir-fry 2 minutes. Serve on hot cooked rice.

*Makes 4 to 6 servings.*

## □ *TUNA PÂTÉ*

**Free of:**
Corn
Egg
Soy
Wheat
Yeast

1 package (8-ounce) cream cheese, softened
1 tablespoon grated onion
3 tablespoons tomato puree
2 tablespoons snipped parsley

2 cans (7 ounces each) water-packed tuna fish, drained and flaked
2 tablespoons milk
salt
raw relishes
crisp crackers

Blend together cream cheese, onion, tomato puree, and parsley. Add tuna fish and milk; mix well. Add salt to taste. Heap in a bowl or make into a ball. Serve with raw relishes or crisp crackers.

*Makes approximately 4 servings or a great many when used as an appetizer.*

## □ *TUNA PIZZA*

**Free of:**
Eggs
Milk
Soy
Wheat
Yeast

1/3 cup olive oil
2 cloves garlic, chopped
4 large onions, chopped
½ teaspoon crumbled oregano
8 corn tortillas

1 can (5¾-ounce drained weight) pitted black olives, drained and halved
1 can (6½-ounce) water-packed chunk tuna, drained

In large skillet, heat olive oil. Sauté garlic and onions unil soft and mushy but not brown. Stir over low heat. Stir in oregano.

Put tortillas on cookie sheets. Spread onions evenly over tortillas. Top with olives and tuna. Bake at 400°F for 20 to 25 minutes or until crusty and brown. Cut into wedges and serve hot.

*Makes 6 to 8 servings.*

## □ TUNA QUICHE

| | | |
|---|---|---|
| 2 9-inch pie shells (PASTRY, FRENCH-STYLE, page 188) | 2 tablespoons lemon juice | **Free of:** |
| | 2 teaspoons onion powder | Corn |
| 2 cans (6 ounces each) tuna (or crabmeat), water-packed, drained | 1 cup cubed Romano cheese | Soy |
| | 1 teaspoon parsley | Yeast |
| | SOUR CREAM CUSTARD (see below) | |

Bake shells and cool. Combine next 5 ingredients; cover and refrigerate at least 2 hours. Cover bottom of shells with cheese-tuna mixture. Cover with SOUR CREAM CUSTARD.

### SOUR CREAM CUSTARD

4 eggs, beaten
½ cup sour cream
1 cup milk
¼ teaspoon salt

Beat together until smooth. Bake at 350°F for 55 minutes until lightly browned and set. Cool slightly.

*Makes 4 servings for a main dish, but may also be served in small wedges as an appetizer.*

## □ *TUNA SKILLET*

**Free of:**
Corn
Egg
Soy
Wheat
Yeast

1¼ cups CREAMED CELERY
   SOUP (pages 269–70)
1½ cups water
1 package (10-ounce) frozen
   green beans

1 large onion, sliced
½ teaspoon garlic powder
1 cup raw rice
2 cans (6½ ounces each) tuna,
   water-packed, drained

Combine soup, water, beans, onion, and garlic powder in large skillet. Cover and bring to a boil. Stir in rice and tuna; cover and simmer 10 minutes or until most of liquid is absorbed.

*Makes 6 to 8 servings.*

# 16

# Recipes for Fruits

## □ APPLE AMBROSIA

½ cup natural unflavored yogurt
1 cup miniature marshmallows
  (egg-free)
3 large apples, cored and diced
  with the skin on

½ cup dry-roasted peanuts,
  salted or plain
½ teaspoon Fruit Fresh or other
  "fruit protector"

**Free of:**
Egg
Soy
Wheat
Yeast

Mix yogurt and marshmallows in medium-size mixing bowl and refrigerate for 1 hour.

Mix remaining ingredients into the yogurt mixture and chill. The "fruit protector" will not alter the flavor of the dish but will prevent the apples from turning brown when exposed to the air.

*Makes 4 ½-cup servings.*

## □ *APPLESAUCE*

**Free of:**
Corn
Egg
Milk
Soy
Wheat
Yeast

Water
16 apples, pared and cored (if
   new apples, do not peel)
1½ lemons for juice
1½ cups sugar (approximately)

1 teaspoon cinnamon
½–1 teaspoon red vegetable
   food coloring (optional)
dash nutmeg

Place apples and juice from lemons in large kettle with 1 to 2 cups water and bring to a boil; boil slowly until practically all the lumps are cooked apart. Add the remaining ingredients and boil gently until sauce is consistency you wish.

*Suggestion:* If possible, use a combination of McIntosh *and* Cortland apples; otherwise, just McIntosh *or* Cortland; or experiment with *good* local cooking apples—*not the green ones.*

*Makes about 3 quarts.*

## □ *CRANBERRY DELIGHT*

**Free of:**
Egg
Soy
Wheat

2 cups fresh cranberries
3 cups miniature marshmallows
   (egg-free)
1–2 cups sugar
2 cups diced apples

½ cup grapes
½ cup broken walnuts
1 cup natural unflavored
   yogurt

Grind cranberries. Mix with marshmallows and sugar. Cover and chill several hours. Add remaining ingredients and fold in yogurt.

*Makes 6 to 8 servings.*

# □ CRANBERRY RELISH

3 cups fresh or frozen cranberries
¾ cup sugar
1 can (8¾-ounce) crushed
  pineapple, packed in water

1½ cups diced apples
½ teaspoon grated lemon peel
3 tablespoons lemon juice

**Free of:**
Corn
Egg
Milk
Soy
Wheat

Put cranberries through coarse blade of a food chopper. Stir in sugar. Drain pineapple and add to cranberries. Add diced apples and remaining ingredients to cranberries. Stir; then refrigerate.

*Makes 1 to 2 quarts.*

# □ FRUIT CASSEROLE

1 can (16-ounce) peach slices in
  own juice, drained (reserve
  ¼ cup juice)
¾ cup CRISPY CINNAMON
  TOPPING (page 153)

1 cup APPLESAUCE (page 208)
2 tablespoons butter
heavy cream, whipped (optional)

**Free of:**
Corn
Egg
Soy
Wheat
Yeast

In greased 1-quart round casserole, layer half the peaches, 2 tablespoons peach juice, 2 tablespoons CRISPY CINNAMON TOPPING, and ½ cup APPLE-SAUCE. Repeat layering. Sprinkle with remaining ½ cup topping. Dot with butter. Bake in preheated 400°F oven for 15 to 20 minutes or until hot. Serve with cream, if desired.

*Makes 4 to 6 servings.*

## □ *HEAVENLY HASH*

**Free of:**
Eggs
Milk
Wheat
Yeast

1 can (8¼-ounce) crushed pineapple in its own juice, drained
2 cups whipped Rich's Rich
   Whip
1 cup miniature marshmallows
   (egg-free)

¼ cup chopped maraschino
   cherries
3 tablespoons Rich's Coffee-
   Rich

Combine ingredients and mix thoroughly. Chill at least 1 hour.

*Makes 6 servings.*


## □ *HOT FRUIT COMPOTE*

**Free of:**
Corn
Egg
Milk
Soy
Wheat

1 large can peach halves in their
   own juice
1 large can pineapple chunks in
   their own juice
1 large can pear halves in their
   own juice
1 recipe CHERRY SAUCE
   (see BLUEBERRY SAUCE,
   page 262)

2 cups pitted red sour pie
   cherries, fresh or frozen
   without sugar or syrup
dried apricots
dried prunes
¼–½ cup sherry

Drain thoroughly peaches, pineapple, and pears. Place a layer of prunes and apricots in bottom of an attractive 9x13-inch baking dish; add peaches, pineapple, pears, CHERRY SAUCE, and sour cherries. Add layer of apricots and prunes. Pour sherry over top.

Bake at 350°F for 1 hour. Serve oven to table.

*Serves 8 to 10 or more.*

# □ *ITALIAN PLUMS*

1 cup sugar
1 cup water
1 cinnamon stick

4 pounds Italian plums, halved
   and pitted

**Free of:**
Corn
Egg
Milk
Soy
Wheat
Yeast

   Place first 3 ingredients in large pot and bring to a boil. Gently place plums in boiling syrup, careful to avoid splashing. Cook 5 minutes. Refrigerate quickly. Rinse cinnamon stick in cool water; dry and store in dry place for use at another time.

*Makes about 4 quarts.*

# □ *LEMON BUNDT MOLD*

2 small cartons Rich's Rich
   Whip
4 packages (3 ounces each)
   lemon-flavored gelatin
3 cups boiling water

2 cups pure lemon juice
½-1 cup sugar
maraschino cherries or fresh
   fruit of choice

**Free of:**
Corn
Egg
Milk
Wheat
Yeast

   Defrost Rich Whip according to carton directions; set aside. Dissolve gelatin in boiling water; add lemon juice and sugar. Whip the Rich Whip until it is stiff, with peaks; fold into gelatin.

   Grease a Bundt pan, pour recipe into pan, and mold in refrigerator until firm. Unmold just before serving onto large platter and garnish with fresh grapes; maraschino cherries; fresh, sliced peaches; fresh strawberries; or fresh blueberries.

*Makes one mold, Bundt-cake size.*

## ▢ *LEMON FRUIT FREEZE*

**Free of:**

Corn
Egg
Soy
Wheat
Yeast

½ cup butter
7 cups Rice Chex cereal
   crushed to 3 cups
1/3 cup sugar
1 can (14-ounce) sweetened
   condensed milk (free of corn
   syrup or corn sugar)

½ cup lemon juice
1 recipe of lemon filling from
   LEMON PIE (pages 193–94)
1 can (17-ounce) fruit cocktail in
   its own juice, well drained
2 cups whipped cream, already
   whipped

In medium saucepan, melt butter; stir in cereal crumbs and sugar. Reserving 1/3 cup for garnish, pat crumbs firmly on bottom of 13x9–inch baking pan. Bake at 300°F for 12 minutes. Cool.

In large bowl, mix sweetened condensed milk and lemon juice. Stir in pie filling and fruit cocktail; pour into prepared pan. Top with whipped topping and crumbs. Freeze 4 hours. Remove from freezer 20 minutes before cutting.

*Makes 8 to 10 servings.*

## ▢ *MOLDED CRANBERRIES*

**Free of:**

Corn
Egg
Milk
Soy
Wheat

3 cups fresh cranberries
¾ cup sugar
1 can (8¾-ounce) crushed
   pineapple in its own juice
2 packages (3 ounces each)
   raspberry-flavored gelatin (or
   other red gelatin)

½ teaspoon grated lemon peel
3 tablespoons lemon juice
1½ cups diced apple

Put cranberries through coarse blade of food chopper. Stir in sugar. Let stand while preparing gelatin.

Drain pineapple and add enough water to its juice to make 2 cups liquid. Heat juice mixture to boiling. Remove from heat. Add gelatin and stir until dissolved. Stir in 1 cup cold water, grated lemon peel, and lemon juice. Chill until very slightly thickened.

Fold in drained pineapple, cranberries, and apple. Pour into 1½-quart mold. Chill several hours until set. Unmold on salad greens.

**For relish:** Omit gelatin and discard juices from canned fruit.

*Makes 8 to 10 servings.*

## □ QUICK FRUIT COMPOTE

| | | |
|---|---|---|
| 1 can (16-ounce) apricot halves in their own juice | 1 medium orange, sliced, and slices halved in their own juice | **Free of:** Corn |
| 1 can (16-ounce) pear halves in their own juice | 1 tablespoon pure vanilla extract sliced almonds | Egg Milk |
| | | Soy |

Wheat
Yeast

Pour juice from apricots and pears into large saucepan. Add orange and vanilla, bring to boil, then simmer 5 to 10 minutes or until flavors are blended. Add apricots, oranges, and pears; heat just until hot. Spoon into serving dishes and sprinkle with almonds. Serve hot.

*Makes 4 to 6 servings.*

## □ STRAWBERRY MARSHMALLOW WHIP

| | | |
|---|---|---|
| 1 package (3-ounce) strawberry gelatin | 1 cup miniature marshmallows (egg- and soy-free) | **Free of:** Egg |
| boiling water | 1 can (8¼-ounce) crushed pine- | Milk |
| cold water | apple in its own juice, | Soy |
| 2 cups frozen Rich's Rich Whip, whipped | drained (do not substitute fresh pineapple) | Wheat Yeast |

Prepare gelatin according to directions on the package. Chill until slightly thickened. With electric mixer on medium speed, beat in 1½ cups Rich Whip; continue beating until well blended. Fold in marshmallows and pineapple. Chill until mixture can be mounded in a pretty serving bowl. Garnish with remaining whipped topping and fresh strawberries.

*Makes 4 to 6 servings.*

## □ *STUFFED APPLES*

**Free of:**    ½ cup sugar

Egg    ½ cup water

Soy    1/3 cup cinnamon candies (Red

Wheat      Hots)

Yeast

8 apples, peeled and cored

1–2 packages (3 ounces each)
    cream cheese, softened

½ cup nuts, chopped

Place sugar, water, and cinnamon bits in pan and bring to a boil. Place apples (a few at a time) into syrup in pan and cook. When fully covered and soft, remove onto serving plate and stuff core with a mixture of cream cheese and nuts. Chill 1 hour before serving.

*Makes 8 servings.*

# 17

# Recipes for Jams/ Jellies

## ☐ PEACH JAM

1½ pounds peaches, peeled and
   pitted
3 tablespoons lemon juice
4 cups sugar

¾ cup water
1 package (1¾ ounces)
   powdered fruit pectin

**Free of:**
Corn
Egg
Milk
Soy
Wheat
Yeast

Crush peaches with fork or potato masher. Measure 2 cups into bowl with juices and lemon juice. Thoroughly mix in sugar. Combine water and pectin in saucepan. Bring to boil and boil 1 minute, stirring constantly. Stir pectin mixture into fruit. Continue stirring 3 minutes.

Ladle quickly into sterilized freezer jars or containers, allowing ¼-inch head space. Seal according to manufacturer's directions. Let stand at room temperature 24 hours. Store in freezer. If used within 2 or 3 weeks, store in refrigerator.

*Makes 2½ pints.*

## □ *PEACH-MARBLE JAM*

*Free of:*
Corn
Egg
Milk
Soy
Wheat
Yeast

Prepare 2½ pints of freezer STRAWBERRY JAM (page 217) and an equal amount of freezer PEACH JAM (page 215) as directed. After stirring 3 minutes, let stand in bowls, covered, at room temperature until almost set. (This may take as long as overnight.) Then layer alternately into prepared jars, for marbled effect. Allow each layer to cool before adding the next. Store freezer containers, covered, in the refrigerator between adding layers. Freeze when the containers are filled.

*Makes about 5 pints.*

## □ *RASPBERRY-PEAR JAM #1*

*Free of:*
Corn
Egg
Milk
Soy
Wheat
Yeast

6 to 8 pears
1-2 baskets fresh raspberries
   (½ to 1 pint)
3 tablespoons lemon or lime
   juice

1 package (1¾-ounce)
   powdered fruit pectin
3¾ cups sugar

Quarter, core, and finely chop pears; mash on the cutting board with fork and pack into measuring cup to get 4 cups. Clean and pick over raspberries and pack into measuring cup to get 1¼ cups.

Combine fruits, lemon or lime juice, and pectin in kettle; bring to boil. Boil 1 minute, stirring; then add sugar all at once. Cook, stirring, until it returns to a boil; boil vigorously 1 minute.

Pour, boiling hot, into hot jars. Adjust caps. Process at simmering 10 to 15 minutes in a boiling-water bath.

*Makes 7 ½-pint jars.*

## □ RASPBERRY-PEAR JAM #2

3 pounds pears
1 package (10 ounce) frozen
　raspberries, thawed, undrained
7½ cups sugar

⅛ teaspoon salt
¼ cup lemon juice
1 tablespoon grated orange rind
½ bottle liquid pectin

**Free of:**
Corn
Egg
Milk
Soy
Wheat
Yeast

Halve, core, and chop pears to measure about 6 cups. Combine all ingredients except pectin in kettle; bring to boil, and boil vigorously 1 minute. Add pectin and boil 1 minute longer.

Pour, boiling hot, into hot jars. Adjust caps. Process at simmering 10 to 15 minutes in a boiling-water bath.

**Variation:** If you reduce amount of sugar to 6 cups, the jam will be of a thinner consistency, and makes a delicious sundae sauce.

*Makes about 9 ½-pint jars.*

## □ STRAWBERRY JAM

1 quart strawberries,
　washed and hulled
4 cups sugar

¾ cup water
1 package (1¾-ounce)
　powdered fruit pectin

**Free of:**
Corn
Egg
Milk
Soy
Wheat
Yeast

Crush berries completely. Measure 2 cups fruit with juices into bowl. Thoroughly mix in sugar.

Combine water and pectin in saucepan. Bring to boil and boil 1 minute, stirring constantly. Stir pectin mixture into fruit; continue stirring 3 minutes.

Ladle quickly into sterilized freezer jars or containers, allowing ¼-inch head space. Seal according to manufacturer's directions. Let stand at room temperature 24 hours. Store in freezer. If used within 2 or 3 weeks, store in refrigerator.

*Makes 2½ pints.*

# Recipes for Meats

## □ BEEF CHINESE

1½ cups cooked beef, in strips
½ sliced onion
2 tablespoons safflower oil
1 cup CREAMED CELERY SOUP
  (pages 269–70)

1 1/3 cups water
1 package (10-ounce) frozen
  green beans
1 can water chestnuts
2 tablespoons pure beef broth
1 cup raw rice

**Free of:**
Corn
Egg
Soy
Wheat
Yeast

Brown beef and onion in oil until tender. Add soup, water, beans, chestnuts, and broth; bring to boil. Add rice; simmer until most of liquid is absorbed.

*Makes 4 to 6 servings.*

## □ *BEEF CURRY*

**Free of:**
Corn
Egg
Soy
Wheat
Yeast

*1 pound already cooked beef,*
*    cut into 1-inch cubes*
*1 cup CREAMED CELERY SOUP*
*    (pages 269–70)*

*1 teaspoon curry powder*
*¼ cup pure beef broth*
*3 cups hot steamed rice*

In skillet or medium-size saucepan, combine beef with soup, curry powder, and beef broth. Heat gently until well blended and hot. Serve over hot steamed rice.

Offer a choice of condiments to sprinkle over curry:
   shredded coconut
   chopped orange sections
   chutney (contains yeast)
   chopped tomatoes
   salted peanuts, dry-roasted
   crumbled bacon
   chopped cucumbers
Condiments may be in small bowls on a tray.

*Note:* In preparing this curry, be sure to take into account the varied strengths of curry powders and your family's preferences. Start with a small amount of curry and gradually increase it to the desired taste.

*Makes 4 to 6 servings.*

## □ *CHOP SUEY*

**Free of:**
Corn
Egg
Milk
Soy
Wheat
Yeast

*1 pound cubed lean round or*
*    chuck steak*
*1 medium onion, finely chopped*
*1 package (10-ounce) frozen green*
*    beans*
*1 package (10-ounce)*
*    frozen pea pods or*
*    snow peas*

*salt to taste*
*1 tablespoon molasses*
*4 ribs fresh celery*
*½ cup green pepper*
*cooked rice for 4 servings*

Brown meat and onion. Add remaining ingredients except pea pods. Simmer covered 1½ hours. Add pea pods and simmer 5 minutes. Serve over hot rice.

*Serves 4.*

## □ *ISRAELI POT ROAST*

| | | Free of: |
|---|---|---|
| *1 5-6-pound pot roast of beef* | *½ cup brown sugar* | Corn |
| *½ teaspoon salt* | *dash ground ginger* | Egg |
| *¼ teaspoon pepper* | *2 cups water* | Milk |
| *¼ cup safflower oil* | *1 tablespoon potato starch* | Soy |
| *4 cups chopped onions (4 large)* | *1 tablespoon water* | Wheat |
| *1 cup lemon juice* | | Yeast |

Toss meat with salt and pepper. Heat oil in heavy kettle over medium heat. Brown meat on all sides; remove and set aside.

Sauté onions in remaining oil; return meat to pan and add lemon juice, sugar, ginger, and 2 cups water. Cover. Bring to a boil. Cook 3 to 3½ hours simmering, or at 350°F in oven. Remove to plate when tender. Keep warm.

Skim fat from liquid. Blend potato starch and 1 tablespoon water and stir into liquid until thickened. Serve this sauce with the sliced roast.

*Makes 8 to 10 servings.*

## □ *MULLIGAN STEW*

| | | Free of: |
|---|---|---|
| *1 tablespoon safflower oil* | *2 cups water* | Corn |
| *1 pound beef, cut into small* | *3 carrots* | Egg |
| *pieces* | *3 potatoes, each cut into 4* | Milk |
| *1 teaspoon salt* | *pieces* | Soy |
| *1 can (10½-ounce) tomato puree* | *2 onions, each cut into 4 pieces* | Wheat |
| | | Yeast |

In a heavy pan or skillet with lid, put oil; add beef and brown over medium heat. Add salt, puree, and water; cover tightly and cook slowly until tender, about 1 hour.

Add carrots, potatoes, and onions; cover, and continue cooking slowly about 30 minutes. If there is not enough liquid, add more water during cooking. If stew is too thin, remove lid and cook until thickened.

*Makes 4 servings.*

## □ *PEPPER STEAK*

**Free of:**
Corn
Egg
Milk
Wheat
Yeast

2 pounds round steak
1/3 cup safflower oil
1 teaspoon salt
dash pepper
dash garlic powder
¼ cup soy sauce

1 sliced green pepper
1 can bean sprouts, drained
1 onion, chopped
2 tomatoes, quartered
1 tablespoon potato starch
steamed rice for 8 servings

Cut meat into paper-thin, finger-length strips. Brown meat in oil in large frying pan. Add seasonings and stir occasionally. Cover and cook over low heat 30 minutes or until tender.

Add soy sauce, green pepper, bean sprouts, and onion. Cover and cook 5 minutes. Add tomatoes. Blend potato starch with ½ cup water and add to meat mixture. Cook, stirring gently, until sauce is thick and clear. Serve with steamed rice.

*Makes 6 to 8 servings.*

## □ PEPPER STEAK SUPREME

2 pounds round steak, cut
    into strips
1/3 cup safflower oil
1 clove garlic, crushed
1 teaspoon salt
dash pepper
¼ teaspoon ginger
¼ cup pure beef broth

2 green peppers, cut into wedges
1 package (10-ounce) frozen
    green beans
1 medium onion, thinly sliced
4 medium tomatoes, quartered
1 tablespoon potato starch
½ cup water
steamed rice for 8 servings

**Free of:**
Corn
Egg
Milk
Soy
Wheat
Yeast

Brown the meat with oil, garlic, salt, pepper, and ginger; stir occasionally. Reduce heat, cover, and simmer for 30 minutes.

Add broth, green pepper, beans, and onion. Cover and cook for 5 minutes. Add tomatoes. Blend potato starch with water and add. Cook, stirring gently until sauce is thickened and clear. Serve with steamed rice.

*Makes 6 servings.*

## □ QUICK BEEF STEW

1½ pounds round steak, about
    ¾ inch thick
3 tablespoons potato starch
1 tablespoon salt
½ teaspoon pepper
¼ cup butter
2 cups carrots, cut in 1-inch
    chunks
2 large onions, sliced

1 large potato, cut in 1-inch
    chunks
1 cup celery
1 bay leaf
3 cups water
1 cup sour cream
2 teaspoons paprika

**Free of:**
Corn
Egg
Soy
Wheat
Yeast

About 45 minutes before serving, cut meat into ¼-inch strips. On waxed paper, combine potato starch, salt, and pepper; coat meat, reserving remaining starch mixture.

In large skillet, over medium-high heat, in melted butter, brown meat well. Add carrots, onions, potato, celery, bay leaf, and 3 cups water. Simmer, covered, over medium heat 30 minutes or until meat and vegetables are fork-tender.

Stir in remaining starch mixture and cook until thickened slightly, stirring constantly. Stir sour cream and paprika into stew; heat, but do not boil.

*Makes 6 servings.*

## □ SMOTHERED STEAK

**Free of:**
Corn
Egg
Soy
Wheat
Yeast

*1½ pounds round steak, about*
*¾ inch thick*
*2 tablespoons safflower oil*
*1 cup CREAMED CELERY SOUP*
*(pages 269–70)*

*1 cup sliced onion*
*1 tablespoon pure beef broth*
*1 teaspoon salt*

Cut meat in serving-size pieces. In skillet, brown meat in oil; then pour off fat. Add soup, onion, broth, and salt. Cover and simmer over low heat 1½ to 2 hours or until tender. Serve with potatoes or rice and cooked vegetables.

*Makes 4 servings.*

## □ SWISS STEAK

**Free of:**
Corn
Egg
Milk
Soy
Wheat
Yeast

*3 pounds boneless chuck (cut in*
*portion pieces 1½ inches thick)*
*1 teaspoon salt*
*½ teaspoon pepper*
*¼ cup potato starch*

*1 large onion, diced*
*2 tablespoons safflower oil*
*1 large can tomatoes with juice*
*pineapple (optional)*

Season meat with salt and pepper, sprinkling potato starch on each side of meat. Then press potato starch into meat with the edge of a saucer. In Dutch oven, brown onion in oil and remove from pan. Brown meat on both sides and cover with onion and tomatoes with juice.

Cook in Dutch oven on top of stove over low heat for 2 hours or until meat is tender. Garnish with pineapple slices packed in own juice or water and small whole potatoes.

*Makes 6 servings.*

## □ *GRANDMA'S CHILI*

| | | |
|---|---|---|
| *1 pound lean ground chuck* | *1 large can red beans* | **Free of:** |
| *1 onion* | *1 large can tomatoes* | *Corn* |
| *1 teaspoon salt* | *1 can (6-ounce) tomato paste* | *Egg* |
| *1 teaspoon chili powder* | | *Milk* |
| | | *Soy* |

Brown meat and onion in large soup pot (2 quarts). Add remaining ingredients. Bring to a boil; then reduce heat to simmer. Cook covered 1 hour, stirring occasionally to avoid burning.

*Wheat*
*Yeast*

*Makes 4 to 6 servings.*

## □ *SUKIYAKI*

| | | |
|---|---|---|
| *2 pounds round steak* | *2 cups sliced onions* | **Free of:** |
| *½ cup soy sauce* | *1 cup sliced celery* | *Corn* |
| *½ cup beef broth* | *1 cup bamboo shoots* | *Egg* |
| *¼ cup red wine* | *1 cup sliced mushrooms* | *Milk* |
| *3 tablespoons sugar* | *1 cup bean sprouts* | *Wheat* |
| *¼ teaspoon pepper* | *White or brown rice or rice* | |
| *¼ cup safflower oil* | *noodles for 8 servings* | |

Cut meat in paper-thin, finger-length slices. Combine soy sauce, broth, wine, sugar, and pepper in small bowl.

Heat oil in frying pan. Brown meat and cook until tender. Then push to side of pan and pour ½ of soy mixture over it. Add onions, celery, bamboo shoots, mushrooms, and bean sprouts; sauté 3 minutes. Pour remaining soy mixture into pan. Cook 5 minutes or until vegetables are tender and crisp. Serve with white or brown rice or rice noodles.

*Makes 6 to 8 servings.*

## □ *BEEF BURGERS*

**Free of:**
Corn
Milk
Soy
Wheat
Yeast

1½ pounds ground beef
¾ cup rolled oats, uncooked
½ cup chopped onion or green
   pepper

1/3 cup tomato puree
1 egg
1 teaspoon salt
⅛ teaspoon pepper

Combine all ingredients; mix well. Shape to form 6 3½-inch patties. Cook in broiler, or over ash-covered coals about 5 inches from heat, 5 to 6 minutes per side or until desired doneness. Serve on hamburger buns, if desired.

*Makes 6 servings.*

## □ *BEEF-RICE SKILLET*

**Free of:**
Corn
Egg
Soy
Wheat
Yeast

1 pound ground beef
1 cup uncooked rice
2½ cups water
2 teaspoons salt
1 cup chopped onion

1 package (3-ounce) cream
   cheese, cubed
1 can (15-ounce) tomato puree
1 teaspoon chili powder

Brown beef in 10-inch skillet; drain. Stir in rice, water, salt, and onion. Bring to boil. Reduce heat, cover, and cook over low heat until water is absorbed, about 25 minutes.

Stir in cubed cheese until it softens. Combine tomato puree and chili powder; pour over rice mixture. Cover and heat 5 minutes or until hot.

**Variations:** Stir in 1/3 cup sliced ripe olives after adding cheese. Add 1 tablespoon diced canned green chiles to cheese-rice mixture and omit chili powder.

*Makes 4 to 6 servings*

## □ *HAMBURGER IN A SKILLET*

| | | Free of: |
|---|---|---|
| 1 pound ground beef | 1 package (10-ounce) frozen peas | |
| 2 cups beef broth | 1 can (5-ounce) water chestnuts | Corn |
| ¼ teaspoon garlic salt | (optional) | Egg |
| 1½ cups water | ½ cup diced onion | Milk |
| 1/3 cup uncooked rice | | Soy |
| | | Wheat |

Brown ground beef and diced onions in a large frying pan; pour off drippings. Blend in beef broth, garlic salt, water, and uncooked rice. Reduce heat to low; cover; simmer 15 minutes. Stir in thawed peas and water chestnuts. Simmer until rice is tender.

Yeast

*Makes 4 to 6 servings.*

## □ *PEANUT BUTTER BURGERS*

| | | Free of: |
|---|---|---|
| | | Corn |
| 2 eggs, slightly beaten | ¼ cup natural chunk-style | Milk |
| 2 pounds ground beef | peanut butter | Soy |
| ½ cup chopped onion | 1 teaspoon salt | Wheat |
| | ¼ teaspoon pepper | Yeast |

Combine all ingredients. Shape into 8 patties. Broil 6 to 7 minutes. Top with dill-pickle slices.

*Makes 8 servings.*

## □ MEATBALLS

**Free of:**
Corn
Milk
Soy
Wheat
Yeast

1½ pounds ground beef
¾ cup rolled oats, uncooked
½ cup chopped green onion or
　green pepper
1/3 cup tomato puree

1 egg
1 teaspoon salt
⅛ teaspoon pepper
2 tablespoons safflower oil

### SAUCE

1 can (8-ounce) tomato puree
1 can (6-ounce) tomato paste
½ cup water

1½ teaspoons oregano leaves,
　crushed
¼ teaspoon salt

For meatballs, combine all ingredients except oil; mix well. Shape to form 16 meatballs. Brown in oil in large skillet; drain.

For sauce, combine all ingredients; mix well. Pour over meatballs in skillet. Cover; simmer about 30 minutes. Serve with salad and French bread or bread sticks, as desired.

*Makes 6 to 8 servings.*

## □ CHEESY BEEF PIE

**Free of:**
Soy
Wheat
Yeast

1 pound ground beef
½ cup chopped onion
1 can (8-ounce) tomato puree
¼ cup snipped parsley
⅛ teaspoon pepper
¼ teaspoon dried oregano,
　crushed

8 corn tortillas, refrigerated and
　uncooked
3 eggs
½ to 1 ounce Romano
　cheese

In skillet, brown beef and onion; drain. Stir in tomato puree, parsley, pepper, and oregano; set aside.

Place 4 tortillas together, filling 9-inch pie plate; trim. Separate one of the eggs; set yolk aside. Beat egg white with remaining two eggs. Spread half over tortilla dough. Spoon meat into shell. Arrange cheese slices atop; spread remaining egg mixture over cheese. Mix reserved yolk and 1 tablespoon water; brush lightly on edge of pastry. Reserve remaining egg-water mixture.

Place remaining 4 tortillas atop filling. Trim and seal with water; cut slits for escape of steam. Brush top with remaining egg-yolk mixture. Bake in 350°F oven for 50 to 55 minutes. If pastry gets too brown, cover with foil. Let stand 10 minutes.

*Makes 6 servings.*

## □ *GROUND-BEEF PIE*

### MEAT-PIE SHELL

| | | |
|---|---|---|
| 1 pound ground beef | 1 egg | **Free of:** |
| 2/3 cup rolled oats (quick or | ¾ teaspoon salt | Corn |
| old-fashioned, uncooked) | ⅛ teaspoon pepper | Soy |
| ½ cup tomato puree | ⅛ teaspoon garlic powder | Wheat |
| ½ cup chopped onion | | Yeast |

### FILLING

1 medium-size zucchini, sliced ¼-inch thick, or 1 package (9-ounce) frozen Italian cut green beans, cooked, drained
1 cup (4 ounces) shredded Romano cheese
½ cup tomato puree
½ cup ripe olive slices
½ teaspoon oregano leaves, crushed
½ teaspoon basil leaves, crushed

For meat-pie shell, combine all ingredients; mix well. Press onto bottom and sides of 9-inch pie plate. Partially bake in preheated oven, 350°F, 8 minutes; drain.

For filling, combine zucchini, ½ cup Romano cheese, tomato puree, olives, and seasoning; spoon into partially baked meat-pie shell. Top with remaining Romano cheese.

Continue baking in 350°F oven for 15 to 18 minutes. Cut into wedges to serve.

*Makes 4 to 6 servings.*

## ◻ *MAMA'S MEAT LOAF*

**Free of:**
Corn
Egg
Milk
Soy
Wheat
Yeast

2 pounds ground chuck
1 cup crisp, ready-to-eat rice cereal
1 onion, grated

1 large can (10-ounce) tomato paste
1 teaspoon salt
¼ teaspoon pepper

Combine ingredients in large bowl, mixing well. Place in loaf pan and bake at 350°F for 1½ hours.

*Makes 6 to 8 servings.*

**Free of:**
Corn
Egg
Milk
Soy
Wheat
Yeast

## ◻ *MEAT LOAF #1*

1½ pounds ground beef
1 cup tomato puree
¾ cup rolled oats, uncooked

½ cup chopped onion or green pepper
1 teaspoon salt
⅛ teaspoon pepper

### BARBECUE SAUCE

| | |
|---|---|
| *1/3 cup tomato puree* | *½ tablespoon dry mustard* |
| *1 tablespoon packed brown* | *powder* |
| *sugar* | *1 tablespoon water* |

Combine first 6 ingredients; mix well. Shape to form 8x4–inch loaf; bake in large, shallow baking pan in preheated oven, 350°F, about 1 hour.

For barbecue-sauce topping, combine ingredients and brush over meat loaf or individual meat loaves during last 10 minutes of baking.

**Variations:** For individual meat loaves, shape meat mixture to form 6 loaves; bake in large, shallow baking pan in preheated, moderate oven, 375°F, for 25 to 30 minutes.

*Makes 6 to 8 servings.*

## □ MEAT LOAF #2

| | | Free of: |
|---|---|---|
| *1½ pounds ground beef (or 1 pound beef and ¼ pound each pork and veal)* | *1 tablespoon dry mustard* | Corn |
| | *2 cloves garlic, minced, or ½ teaspoon garlic powder* | Milk |
| *1 cup water* | *½ teaspoon sage* | Soy |
| *1 cup coarse oatmeal* | *½ teaspoon thyme* | Wheat |
| *¾ cup unprocessed rice bran* | *1 teaspoon salt* | Yeast |
| *1 egg* | *¼ teaspoon pepper* | |
| *½ cup tomato puree* | *2 teaspoons safflower oil* | |

Mix all ingredients. Pack in 9x5x3–inch loaf pan. Bake in 350°F oven 1¼ to 1½ hours.

*Makes 6 servings.*

## □ *PIZZA*

**Free of**:
Egg
Soy
Wheat
Yeast

8 corn tortillas (approximately 6 inches in diameter)
1 can (6-ounce) tomato paste
1 pound lean ground meat, browned and broken into crumbs

¾ cup grated Romano cheese
½ cup chopped onions
½ cup chopped green pepper
oregano, salt, and pepper to taste

Put 4 tortillas each on two cookie sheets, spacing them evenly apart. Divide each ingredient among the 8 tortillas, layering first the tomato paste, then meat, ½ cup Romano, onions, green pepper, seasonings, and rest of Romano. Bake at 350°F for 20 minutes or until cheese is bubbly and golden.

*Makes 8 pizzas, 6 inches each.*

## □ *TACOS*

**Free of**:
Eggs
Soy
Wheat
Yeast

2 pounds ground beef
1 small onion, finely chopped
1 cup water
2 cans (6 ounces) tomato paste
1 teaspoon chili powder
¼ teaspoon garlic powder

½ medium-size iceberg lettuce
1 large avocado
2 large tomatoes, fresh
1 can (7¼-ounce) pitted ripe olives
8 ounces shredded Romano cheese
12 crisp corn tortillas

In 12-inch skillet, over high heat, cook ground beef and

RECIPES FOR MEATS □ 233

onion until meat is well browned, stirring frequently. Stir in water, tomato paste, and spices; heat to boiling. Reduce heat to medium-low; simmer 10 minutes. Meanwhile, shred lettuce; dice avocado and tomatoes; slice olives. Place these and cheese in individual small bowls for serving.

Spoon beef mixture into large bowl; place on platter; arrange corn tortillas and accompaniments around bowl. Let each person help himself by placing tortillas on plate, topping with beef, then accompaniments.

*Makes 6 servings.*

# □ *CHOPPED LIVER (PÂTÉ)*

| | | |
|---|---|---|
| 1 pound calf's liver or chicken livers | 3 hard-cooked eggs | **Free of:** |
| 2 onions, sliced | 1 teaspoon salt | Corn |
| 6 tablespoons rendered chicken fat or safflower oil | ¼ teaspoon pepper | Milk |
| | | Soy |
| | | Wheat |
| | | Yeast |

Gently sauté liver and onions in the 2 tablespoons of chicken fat or oil. When liver is no longer pink, remove liver and onions from pan and cool.

Grind liver, onions, and eggs together. Add the 4 tablespoons fat or oil, salt, and pepper and mix together thoroughly.

Chill in bowl or mold. Turn out on a platter and serve with RyKrisp or rice crackers, or serve mounded on a lettuce leaf for individual first courses.

**Variation:** Create elegant liver pâté in Danish-pastry croûte by combining dough (see recipe for DANISH

CHEESE PASTRIES) with a filling of this pâté. Completely enclose the filling and bake as directed. Slice and serve hot.

*Makes 12 to 14 servings.*

## □ *LAMB CHOPS WITH HONEY GLAZE*

**Free of:**
Corn
Egg
Milk
Soy
Wheat
Yeast

4–6 large shoulder lamb
    chops, ¾ inch thick
salt and pepper to taste
2 tablespoons safflower oil
½ teaspoon curry powder
½ cup fresh orange juice

2 tablespoons fresh
    lemon juice
4 tablespoons honey
1 can (11-ounce) water-
    packed mandarin oranges,
    drained

Sprinkle chops with salt and pepper. Score fat around edges of chops to prevent curling. Brown both sides well under broiler. Drain off all fat.

Place in oiled baking pan. Combine curry powder, orange juice, lemon juice, and honey. Pour over chops and bake in a preheated 350°F oven 30 to 45 minutes. Add oranges to sauce for last 5 minutes, to warm them.

*Makes 4 to 6 servings.*

## □ *LAMB CHOPS SPECIAL*

**Free of:**
Corn
Egg
Milk
Soy
Wheat
Yeast

4–6 round bone shoulder
    lamb chops
1 can (1-pound) whole tomatoes
1 onion, chopped
1 green pepper, cut in
    square chunks

1 teaspoon salt
½ teaspoon sugar
1 teaspoon dried oregano
1 clove garlic, minced

Score fat around edges of chops to prevent curling. Brown both sides well under broiler. Drain off all fat. In the broiler pan, combine tomatoes, onions, green pepper, salt, sugar, oregano, and garlic. Place chops on top and bake in a preheated 350°F oven 30 to 45 minutes, until chops are tender.

**Variation:**   Sliced zucchini may be added during the last 10 minutes of baking if desired.

*Makes 4 to 6 servings.*

## □ LAMB PILAF

| | | |
|---|---|---|
| 3 pounds boned lamb | 2 teaspoons salt | **Free of:** |
| 2 tablespoons safflower oil | 1 cup beef stock | Corn |
| 1 large onion, sliced | 2 cups water | Egg |
| ½ teaspoon cinnamon | ¼ cup lemon juice | Milk |
| ½ teaspoon freshly | 1 cup slivered | Soy |
| ground pepper | almonds | Wheat |
| 2 cups raw white rice | 3 tablespoons snipped | |
| 1 cup white raisins | parsley | |

Cut lamb in 1-inch cubes. Sauté lamb in safflower oil over high heat until brown. Remove lamb as it browns and drain on paper toweling.

After all lamb is browned, lower heat to medium and sauté onion, cinnamon, and pepper for 3 to 5 minutes.

In a greased casserole, sprinkle about ½ cup rice, to cover bottom. Make layer of rice, raisins, meat, and onions. Repeat until all are used up. Sprinkle top with salt. Combine stock and water and pour over the mixture in the casserole.

Cover and bake in a preheated 400°F oven for 60

minutes. Remove cover, sprinkle with lemon juice and almonds, and bake for 10 more minutes. Add parsley just before serving.

*Makes 8 to 10 servings.*

## □ *LEG OF LAMB WITH MUSTARD*

**Free of:**
Corn
Egg
Milk
Soy
Wheat
Yeast

1 tablespoon dry mustard powder in ¼ cup water
1 teaspoon rosemary or thyme
¼ teaspoon powdered ginger
2 tablespoons pure beef stock

2 tablespoons safflower oil
1 6–8-pound leg of lamb
1 garlic clove, slivered

Blend sauce of mustard, herbs, ginger, and beef stock in a bowl. Beat in oil, to make a creamy mixture.

Make 4 shallow slashes in the meat with a sharp knife and tuck into each a sliver of garlic. Brush lamb liberally with sauce and let stand for 1 to 2 hours. Roast on a rack in a preheated 350°F oven for 1¼ to 1½ hours.

*Makes 4 to 6 servings.*

# 19

# *Recipes for Pancakes/ Waffles*

## ☐ *PEANUT BUTTER PANCAKES*

¾ cup oat flour
¼ cup dry milk powder
 (1/3 cup instant)
½ teaspoon salt
2 teaspoons corn-free
 baking powder
2 eggs, beaten

¼ cup honey
½ teaspoon pure
 vanilla extract
½ cup natural peanut
 butter
¼ cup water

**Free of:**
Corn
Soy
Wheat
Yeast

In mixing bowl, stir together flour, milk powder, salt, and baking powder. Make a "hole" in the middle of the dry ingredients and add eggs, honey, vanilla, peanut butter, and water. Beat well, mixing into dry ingredients until batter is smooth. Bake on a hot, oiled grill or skillet. For waffles, use same ingredients, but only 1 cup water.

*Makes enough pancakes for 1 to 2 people, depending on their appetites and the accompanying dishes.*

## ◻ POTATO PANCAKES

**Free of:**
Corn
Milk
Soy
Wheat
Yeast

4 large potatoes,
   peeled and cubed
2 eggs
1 teaspoon salt
¼ teaspoon corn-free
   baking powder

⅛ teaspoon pepper
1 small onion (optional)
safflower oil for
   frying
¼ cup potato starch

In blender, combine all ingredients except potato starch. Blend until lumps are gone. Add starch. Blend until thoroughly mixed. Fry in safflower oil until crisp and golden. Drain on paper toweling. Serve with applesauce or meat.

*Makes enough pancakes for 4 main-dish servings or 6 to 8 servings when served with an entrée.*

## ◻ SUNFLOWER-ROLLED WAFFLES

**Free of:**
Corn
Soy
Wheat
Yeast

2 cups rolled oats
6 cups boiling water
6 tablespoons dry milk
   powder
1 egg
2 tablespoons honey

2 tablespoons safflower oil
¼ teaspoon salt
2/3 cup sunflower seeds
2 teaspoons potato starch

Put oats in a medium bowl and pour in boiling water. Stir and let sit for 2 minutes. Beat in remaining ingredients. Fry in hot waffle iron according to manufacturer's instructions.

*Makes 1 to 2 servings.*

# Recipes for Pasta

## ☐ *RICOTTA SAUCE WITH PASTA*

½ pound uncooked rice
   noodles
¾ cup cottage cheese
2 ounces Romano
   cheese, grated

1 tablespoon butter
salt, nutmeg, fresh-
   ground pepper

**Free of:**
Corn
Egg
Soy
Wheat
Yeast

Cook rice noodles according to package directions. Drain well. Add remaining ingredients and mix well. Serve hot with salad or brightly colored cooked vegetables.

*Makes 2 to 3 servings.*

## □ *ZUCCHINI SAUCE FOR PASTA*

**Free of:**

Corn
Egg
Milk
Soy
Wheat
Yeast

3 tablespoons safflower oil
3 medium zucchini or
    other summer squash,
    diced
1 small onion, diced
1 green pepper, diced
2 teaspoons salt

1½ teaspoons sugar
½ teaspoon oregano
1 can (16-ounce)
    tomato puree
1 pound rice noodles,
    cooked according to
    package directions

In large skillet, over medium heat, place oil and add zucchini or squash and onion. Cook until tender. Add rest of ingredients and cook until mixture is heated. Serve over noodles.

**Variation:** Add 2 pounds ground meat, browned, or meatballs when zucchini or squash is cooked. Brown meat and continue with the original recipe.

*Makes 6 servings.*

## □ *SPAGHETTI SAUCE PLUS*

**Free of:**

Corn
Egg
Milk
Soy
Wheat
Yeast

1 onion, chopped
½ green pepper, chopped
¼ teaspoon garlic
    powder
¼ teaspoon pepper
½–1 teaspoon oregano

1 pound rice noodles,
    cooked according to
    directions on the package
1 large can tomato paste
1 large can stewed tomatoes
1 large can tomato puree

Brown onion, green pepper, garlic powder, pepper, and oregano. Add paste, tomatoes, and puree. Simmer at least ½ hour. Serve over hot noodles.

*Makes approximately 2 quarts of sauce.*

## Variations:

**Meat sauce:** Brown 1 pound ground meat with onion. Serve over noodles.

**Sweet-and-sour sauce:** Add 1 can whole-berry cranberry sauce. Bring basic sauce to boil in large pot. Add raw chicken parts. Simmer 2 hours on top of stove or until chicken is soft. Serve over rice. (This variation is not yeast-free.)

**With chicken:** Bone chicken breasts. Bread with crumbs of ready-to-eat crisp rice cereal. Fry in safflower oil on both sides until golden. Bake in shallow pan at 350°F for ½ hour. Pour 1 small can tomato sauce over top. Sprinkle with Parmesan or mozzarella cheese. Bake until cheese melts. (This variation is not milk-free.)

## □ LASAGNA

| | | Free of: |
|---|---|---|
| 1 pound cottage cheese | ½ pound lasagna-style | Corn |
| 1 egg | rice noodles | Soy |
| salt to taste | 1 quart SPAGHETTI SAUCE | Wheat |
| pepper to taste | PLUS (See previous recipe.) | Yeast |
| 8 ounces grated | 1 small green pepper, diced | |
| Romano cheese | | |

In blender, combine cottage cheese, egg, salt, and pepper. Cook pasta as directed. Add diced green pepper to meat sauce.

In 9x12–inch pan, layer noodles, meat sauce, cottage cheese, then Romano cheese. Repeat.

Bake at 350°F for 30 minutes. Let stand 10 minutes before serving.

*Makes 6 to 8 servings.*

## □ *SPINACH-STUFFED SHELLS*

**Free of:**
Corn
Egg
Soy
Yeast

1 package (12-ounce)
   jumbo macaroni shells
2 cups chopped spinach
1 container (15-ounce)
   cottage cheese
1 cup Romano
   cheese, shredded

1 teaspoon salt
¼ teaspoon pepper
½ pound ground beef
1 quart SPAGHETTI SAUCE
   PLUS (pages 240-241)

About 1½ hours before serving:

Prepare macaroni shells as label directs; drain well. Cook spinach and drain well; put into a large bowl and cool slightly. Stir in cottage cheese, Romano, salt, and pepper. Stuff each shell with a tablespoonful of mixture. Arrange about 4 shells in each of 10 individual casseroles.

In 10-inch skillet over medium heat, cook ground beef until browned, stirring frequently. Stir in spaghetti sauce. Spoon a scant 1/3 sauce evenly over each casserole; cover with foil. Freeze casseroles, to be served later. Bake remaining casseroles in 350°F oven 30 minutes or until bubbly.

Serve frozen casseroles within 3 months. About 1 hour before serving, preheat oven to 350°F. Bake frozen covered casseroles about 30 minutes or until bubbly.

*Makes 10 servings.*

# Recipes for Poultry

## □ *CHICKEN ALMOND*

3 cups cooked chicken
  (4 double chicken breasts)
3 tablespoons safflower oil
2 cups celery, cut in
  ½-inch slices
2½ cups pure chicken
  stock

4 tablespoons potato starch
1 teaspoon sugar
½ cup water
1 or 2 packages frozen
  Chinese pea pods, thawed
  and drained
½ cup whole almonds

**Free of:**
Corn
Egg
Milk
Soy
Wheat
Yeast

Heat chicken in hot oil until golden brown. Add celery and chicken stock. Cook a few minutes.

In a small bowl, mix together potato starch, sugar, and water. Add to chicken mixture and simmer until thickened, stirring constantly.

Add pea pods and almonds; continue stirring. Simmer just until mixture is heated through; do not overcook. Serve over rice.

*Makes 6 to 8 servings.*

## □ *CHICKEN CASSEROLE*

**Free of:**
Corn
Egg
Soy
Wheat
Yeast

2 cups cooked chicken, diced
1 package (10-ounce)
   frozen mixed vegetables
   (no corn)

½ cup diced onion
1 cup CREAMED CELERY
   SOUP (pages 269-70)
½ cup milk

Combine chicken, thawed vegetables, soup, onion, and milk. Pour into 1½-quart casserole. Cover. Bake at 375°F for 45 minutes.

*Makes 4 or 5 servings.*

## □ *CHICKEN CASSEROLE WITH RICE*

**Free of:**
Corn
Egg
Soy
Wheat
Yeast

1¼ cups raw rice
1 cup CREAMED CELERY
   SOUP (pages 269-70)
1 cup pure chicken stock
¼ cup safflower oil

10 to 12 pieces of chicken
   (legs, thighs, or breasts)
½ cup slivered almonds
1/3 cup grated Romano
   cheese

Pour oil in bottom of a 3-quart baking dish and sprinkle rice over the bottom. In a bowl, combine soup and stock. Spread ½ cup of soup mixture over the rice. Place chicken in single layer on top of soup. Spread the remaining ½ cup of soup mixture over chicken.

Bake covered in a preheated 350°F oven for 1 hour. Remove cover and bake 1 hour longer. Sprinkle with almonds and cheese the last 15 to 20 minutes of baking time.

*Makes 4 to 6 servings.*

## □ *CHICKEN WITH A CRUST*

1½ cups oat flour
¾ cup grated Romano
  cheese
½ teaspoon paprika or sage
½ teaspoon salt
¼ teaspoon pepper

1/3 cup milk
1 egg
1 2½-3-pound broiler-
  fryer, cut up
¼ cup butter, melted

**Free of:**
Corn
Soy
Wheat
Yeast

Combine dry ingredients in a shallow bowl. Combine milk and egg in a small bowl. Coat chicken with combined dry ingredients; dip into combined milk and egg. Coat again with dry ingredients. Place in foil-lined, large, shallow baking pan; drizzle melted butter over chicken.

Bake in preheated, hot oven, 400°F, 45 to 50 minutes or until tender and golden brown.

*Makes 4 servings.*

## □ *CHICKEN DIVINE*

1 pound cooked asparagus
  spears or broccoli
  (fresh or frozen)
1-2 pounds sliced cooked
  chicken or turkey
1 cup CREAMED CELERY
  SOUP (pages 269-70)

½ cup cream
½ cup pure chicken stock
½ cup grated Romano
  cheese
1 tablespoon butter, cut
  into dots
paprika

**Free of:**
Corn
Egg
Soy
Wheat
Yeast

Place cooked vegetable on the bottom of a greased, shallow, flat-bottomed casserole. Lay chicken slices on top, overlapping them.

In a saucepan, mix soup, cream, stock, and half of the cheese. Cook over low heat until smooth and well blended, stirring constantly.

Pour sauce over the chicken, covering completely. Top with remaining Romano cheese, dot with butter, sprinkle lightly with paprika.

Bake in a preheated 450°F oven until golden brown on top, about 15 minutes.

*Makes 4 servings.*

## □ *CHICKEN ORIENTALE*

**Free of:**
Corn
Egg
Milk
Soy
Wheat
Yeast

½ cup pure chicken stock
2 cloves garlic, minced
1 teaspoon ginger
2 tablespoons safflower oil

½ teaspoon salt
¼ teaspoon pepper
1–2 frying chickens, quartered (removing skin is optional)

Mix chicken stock, garlic, ginger, oil, salt, and pepper. Pour over the chicken in 9x13x2–inch baking dish. If time allows, chicken can marinate all day in the refrigerator; or marinade can be mixed and poured over the chicken just before baking.

Bake chicken in a 350°F oven for 1 hour and 30 minutes. It will be crispy and very brown.

*Makes 4 to 6 servings.*

# □ *CHICKEN OVEN-FRIED #1*

3½ cups ready-to-
    eat crisp rice cereal,
    crushed
1/3 cup safflower oil
2 teaspoons salt
1 teaspoon paprika

1 tablespoon celery salt
½ teaspoon pepper
½ teaspoon sage (optional)
1 2-3-pound frying chicken,
    cut in pieces

**Free of:**
Corn
Egg
Milk
Soy
Wheat
Yeast

Mix cereal crumbs, oil, and spices together in a shallow bowl. Dip cut-up chicken pieces into crumbs when still wet from rinsing. Place skin side down in baking dish. Bake at 375°F for 45 minutes; then turn pieces skin side up. Bake an additional 30 to 45 minutes until crust is golden.

This recipe is large enough to coat *two* 2–3 pound frying chickens. Leftover crumbs may be refrigerated and used at another time.

# □ *CHICKEN OVEN-FRIED #2*

¼ cup safflower oil
½ teaspoon paprika
1 cup instant
    mashed-potato flakes

1 teaspoon onion salt
1 2-3-pound frying chicken,
    cut in pieces

**Free of:**
Corn
Egg
Milk
Soy
Wheat
Yeast

Preheat oven to 400°F. Pour oil in 9x13–inch pan. In a plastic bag, combine potato flakes and seasonings. Rinse chicken pieces and shake in plastic bag to coat. Remove from bag and place chicken skin side down in oil.

Bake 60 minutes, turning chicken over after 30 minutes. Refrigerate leftovers.

*Makes 4 to 6 servings.*

## □ *CHICKEN PAPRIKASH*

**Free of:**
Corn
Egg
Soy
Wheat
Yeast

1-2 fryers, cut up
1½ cups CREAMED CELERY
 SOUP (pages 269–70)
½–1 cup milk

paprika
cooked rice for
 6 servings
vegetables

Arrange chicken in 9x13x2–inch baking pan. Mix soup with milk and pour over top. Sprinkle with paprika. Bake 1½ hours at 350°F. Serve with rice and cooked green vegetables.

*Makes 4 to 6 servings.*

## □ *CHICKEN SALAD GRANDE*

**Free of:**
Corn
Egg
Soy
Wheat
Yeast

1 teaspoon olive oil
4 cups diced
 cooked chicken
½ cup celery, chopped
2 cups seedless grapes
½ teaspoon salt
½ teaspoon pepper

1 cup SOUR CREAM
 DRESSING (pages 259–60)
½ teaspoon dry mustard
 powder mixed with a few
 drops water to form a paste
½ cup salted pecan
 halves or toasted almonds,
 dry-roasted

Sprinkle chicken with 1 teaspoon olive oil. Combine chicken, celery, grapes, salt, and pepper and toss lightly with SOUR CREAM DRESSING and mustard. Add nuts.

*Makes 6 to 8 servings.*

## □ *CHICKEN STIR-FRY*

| | | |
|---|---|---|
| 2 *whole chicken* | ½ *cup water* | **Free of:** |
| *breasts, boned* | 1 *teaspoon salt* | *Corn* |
| 2 *tablespoons safflower oil* | ½ *teaspoon ground ginger* | *Egg* |
| 1 *medium-size green pepper,* | 4 *teaspoons potato starch* | *Milk* |
| *cut into thin strips* | 2 *tablespoons pure* | *Soy* |
| 1 *small onion, thinly sliced* | *chicken broth* | *Wheat* |
| 1 *cup celery, thinly sliced* | 1 *can (16-ounce) bean* | *Yeast* |
| 1 *can (5-ounce) water* | *sprouts* | |
| *chestnuts, drained* | *cooked rice for* | |
| *and sliced* | 6 *servings* | |

Remove skin and cut chicken into thin strips. Heat oil in a large skillet; add chicken and cook over moderate heat, about 250°F, 4 or 5 minutes or until meat turns white.

Add green pepper, onion, celery, water chestnuts, water, salt, and ginger; cover and cook over moderately low heat, about 225°F, 5 minutes.

Blend potato starch and broth together; stir into chicken mixture. Add bean sprouts and cook about 2 minutes more, or until thickened, stirring constantly. Serve over cooked rice.

*Makes 4 to 6 servings.*

## □ *CHICKEN WITH MUSHROOMS*

| | | |
|---|---|---|
| 4 *whole chicken* | ¼ *teaspoon pepper* | **Free of:** |
| *breasts* | 1 *tablespoon lemon juice* | *Corn* |
| *water* | ½ *pound mushrooms, sliced* | *Egg* |
| ¼ *cup safflower oil* | ¾ *cup dry vermouth* | *Milk* |
| 1 *clove garlic, minced* | ¼ *cup snipped parsley* | *Soy* |
| 1 *teaspoon salt* | | *Wheat* |

Simmer chicken breasts in water to cover until tender enough to remove from bones. Sauté in oil. Add garlic, salt, pepper, and lemon juice. Heap mushrooms on top, pour in vermouth, cover, and cook for 20 to 30 minutes or until chicken is fork-tender. Add a little more vermouth if needed. Sprinkle with parsley just before serving.

*Makes 6 servings.*

# Recipes for Rice Dishes/ Pilafs

## ☐ *APPLE-RICE PUDDING WITH MERINGUE*

4 cups cooked rice

3 cups peeled and
   chopped cooking apples

1 tablespoon grated
   lemon peel

4 eggs, separated

3 cups half-and-half

1 teaspoon pure vanilla
   extract

¾ teaspoon salt

1 cup sugar

**Free of:**

Corn

Soy

Wheat

Yeast

About 2½ hours before serving, or early the same day, combine first 3 ingredients in 2½-quart casserole. In bowl, mix egg yolks, half-and-half, vanilla, salt, and ¾ cup sugar; pour over rice mixture. Set 13x9–inch baking pan on oven rack; place casserole in pan and fill pan halfway with very hot tap water. Bake in 350°F oven 2 hours or until knife inserted in center comes out clean.

252 □ THE ALLERGY COOKBOOK & FOOD-BUYING GUIDE

Carefully remove casserole from pan in oven. In small bowl, with mixer at high speed, beat egg whites until soft peaks form. Gradually sprinkle in ¼ cup sugar, beating well after each addition. Spread whites over rice mixture, making sure that whites touch edge of casserole. Pull up points with back of spoon to make attractive top. Place casserole in same pan of water; bake at 350°F 10 minutes or until top is golden. Serve warm or cool on wire rack; refrigerate.

*Makes 10 servings.*

## □ CHICKEN FRIED RICE

**Free of:**
Corn
Milk
Soy
Wheat
Yeast

1 pound boned chicken breasts
½ cup chopped green pepper
1 cup beef broth

1 cup thinly sliced onions
4 eggs, beaten
3 cups cooked rice

Cut chicken and green pepper in paper-thin slices. In deep skillet, combine broth and celery. Bring to a boil and add chicken, green pepper, and onions. Cook over a low heat 5 to 10 minutes or until chicken is cooked. Stir in eggs, stirring once or twice. Cook until eggs are set. Divide rice among 4 deep plates and spoon chicken mixture over it.

*Makes 4 servings.*

## □ CHINESE FRIED RICE

| | | Free of: |
|---|---|---|
| 3 tablespoons safflower oil | ½ teaspoon pepper | Corn |
| 1 cup cooked chicken, shrimp, or leftover meat | 3 cups cooked, cold rice | Milk |
| 2 eggs, slightly beaten | 2 tablespoons pure beef or chicken stock | Soy |
| ¾ teaspoon salt | 2 green onions, snipped | Wheat |
| | | Yeast |

Heat oil in deep frying pan. Add chicken, meat, or shrimp and cook 1 minute. Add eggs, salt, and pepper, and cook, stirring constantly, until well mixed. Add rice and beef or chicken stock and cook, stirring constantly, for about 5 minutes, until rice is thoroughly heated. To serve, garnish with green onions.

*Makes 4 to 6 servings.*

## □ OAT PILAF

| | | Free of: |
|---|---|---|
| 1½ cups rolled oats, uncooked | ¾ cup pure beef or chicken broth | Corn |
| 2 tablespoons safflower oil | ¼ teaspoon salt | Egg |
| | | Milk |
| | | Soy |
| | | Wheat |
| | | Yeast |

Combine oats and oil in 10-inch skillet; cook over medium heat, stirring constantly, 3 to 5 minutes or until oats are dry, separated, and lightly browned. Add broth and salt; continue cooking, stirring occasionally, 2 to 3 minutes or until liquid evaporates. Serve in place of rice or pasta.

*Makes 4 servings.*

## □ OAT PILAF AND HERBS

**Free of:** 1½ cups rolled oats,                    2 tablespoons dried
Corn          uncooked                              parsley flakes
Milk          1 egg, beaten                         ½ teaspoon oregano leaves
Soy           2 tablespoons safflower oil           ½ teaspoon basil leaves
Wheat         ¾ cup pure chicken or                 ¼ teaspoon salt
Yeast            beef broth

Combine oats and egg in medium-size bowl; mix until oats are thoroughly coated. Add oat mixture to oil in 10- to 12-inch skillet. Cook over medium heat, stirring constantly, 3 to 5 minutes or until oats are dry, separated, and lightly browned. Add remaining ingredients, continue cooking, stirring occasionally, 2 to 3 minutes or until liquid evaporates. Serve in place of rice or pasta.

**Variations:**  Sauté ½ to 1 cup zucchini or green-onion slices or chopped green pepper, spinach, broccoli, or tomatoes in safflower oil in 10- to 12-inch skillet. Add oats and egg mixture.

*Makes 4 servings.*

## □ RICE AND MUSHROOM CASSEROLE

**Free of:**
Corn
Egg        1 small onion, diced              1 tablespoon safflower oil
Milk       ½ medium green pepper,            1½ cups pure beef broth
Soy           diced                         1 cup uncooked rice
Wheat      ½ pound fresh mushrooms

Sauté onion, green pepper, and mushrooms in 1 tablespoon of safflower oil until brown. Combine broth, rice, and browned vegetables in 1½- to 2-quart buttered casserole.

Bake at 350°F until all liquid is absorbed, about 25 minutes.

*Makes 4 servings.*

## □ WILD RICE STUFFING

| | | |
|---|---|---|
| ¼ cup chopped onions | ¼ teaspoon sage | **Free of:** |
| ½ cup chopped celery | ¼ teaspoon thyme | Corn |
| 2 tablespoons safflower oil | ½ teaspoon salt | Egg |
| 2 cups cooked wild rice | | Milk |
| | | Soy |
| | | Wheat |
| | | Yeast |

In large skillet, sauté onions and celery in oil until transparent; add wild rice and seasonings. Mix thoroughly. Serve immediately.

This recipe is enough for stuffing a 4-pound fowl. It may also be baked in a greased 1-quart casserole for 30 minutes at 350°F and served as an accompaniment for beef or poultry dishes.

# Recipes for
# Salad Dressings

## ☐ *BLENDER MAYONNAISE*

1 egg
½ teaspoon salt
½ teaspoon dry mustard
  powder

¼ teaspoon paprika
2 tablespoons lemon juice
1 cup safflower oil

**Free of:**
Corn
Milk
Soy
Wheat
Yeast

Put egg, seasonings, lemon juice, and ¼ cup of oil in blender. Cover and set dial at "blend." Immediately remove feeder cap and pour in remaining oil in a steady, slow stream. Use rubber spatula if necessary to keep ingredients flowing.

Store in covered jar in refrigerator. Mix well before using if ingredients have separated.

*Makes 1¼ cups.*

## □ *CREAMY DRESSING*

**Free of:**
Corn
Egg
Soy
Wheat
Yeast

½ cup cottage cheese
⅛ cup milk
⅛ teaspoon garlic powder
⅛ teaspoon freshly ground
   pepper

⅛ teaspoon dry mustard
1 tablespoon minced onion
¼ teaspoon salt
⅛ teaspoon basil (optional)
⅛ teaspoon thyme (optional)

Place all ingredients in the small jar of an electric blender and blend at low speed until creamy. Refrigerate in covered jar and use within a few days.

*Makes about 1 cup dressing.*

## □ *CREAMY MAYONNAISE*

**Free of:**
Corn
Egg
Milk
Soy
Wheat
Yeast

3 teaspoons powdered
   egg replacer
2 tablespoons water
1 cup safflower oil

1 teaspoon sugar
1 teaspoon salt
2 teaspoons dry mustard
   powder

In small bowl, combine egg replacer and water. Beat with electric mixer until peaks are formed. Add other ingredients very slowly, one at a time, beating continuously.

*Makes about 1½ cups egg-free mayonnaise.*

**Free of:**
Corn
Egg
Milk
Soy
Wheat
Yeast

## □ *ITALIAN DRESSING*

¾ cup olive oil
½ cup lemon juice
2 tablespoons sugar

1 teaspoon garlic powder
1 teaspoon salt
¼ teaspoon pepper

Combine all ingredients in small jar or bottle and chill in refrigerator. Shake well before using. Serve over salad or salad greens and fresh vegetables.

*Makes about 1 cup dressing.*

## □ *ONION DRESSING*

| | | Free of: |
|---|---|---|
| 8 ounces natural unflavored yogurt | ½ teaspoon sugar | Corn |
| 2 tablespoons finely chopped onion | 1 teaspoon salt | Egg |
| ½ teaspoon minced garlic | ¼ teaspoon crumbled oregano | Soy |
| | 1/16 teaspoon white pepper | Wheat |
| | | Yeast |

Combine all ingredients in small bowl and mix thoroughly. Chill in refrigerator. Keeps 1 week.

*Makes 1 cup dressing.*

## □ *SOUR CREAM DRESSING*

| | | Free of: |
|---|---|---|
| ½ cup sour cream | ¾ teaspoon salt | Corn |
| 1 tablespoon milk | 1 tablespoon paprika | Egg |
| ½ teaspoon onion powder | | Soy |

Combine all ingredients in a small bowl and chill in refrigerator. Keeps 1 week. Wheat

This salad dressing is also good when served as a dip Yeast with carrot sticks, cucumber slices, celery, cauliflower flowerettes, and cherry tomatoes.

*Makes about ½ cup dressing.*

## □ *TANGY SOUR CREAM DRESSING*

**Free of:**
Corn
Egg
Soy
Wheat
Yeast

1 cup sour cream
¼ teaspoon salt
celery salt to taste

1½ teaspoons lemon juice
¼ cup honey
½ teaspoon dry mustard

Combine all ingredients in small jar, cover, and chill in refrigerator. Serve with salad of tossed green vegetables.

*Makes about 1¼ cups dressing.*

# Recipes for Sauces/ Gravies

## □ SAUCE ADRIENNE

1 cup BLENDER MAYON-
NAISE (pages 257)
1 teaspoon horseradish

½ teaspoon salt
¾ cup tomato puree

**Free of:**
Corn
Milk
Soy
Wheat
Yeast

Mix all ingredients until well blended. Chill.

## □ *BLUEBERRY SAUCE*

**Free of:**
Corn
Egg
Milk
Soy
Wheat
Yeast

1 tablespoon potato
   starch
2 tablespoons sugar

1 can water-packed
   blueberries, drained
   (save juice)
1 tablespoon fresh
   lemon juice

In medium saucepan, blend potato starch and sugar. Slowly stir in blueberry juice and cook, stirring constantly, over low heat until clear. Add lemon juice and berries, stirring just to mix. Remove from heat immediately and cool.

Serve over blintzes or ice cream or as topping for cheesecake and cream pie. However, it will not be milk-free.

*Variations:* This recipe may be used with any other fruit canned in its own juice: sliced apples, cherries, pineapple, peaches, etc.

*Note:* Allergens listed apply *only* to sauce, not to the foods with which it can be used.

## □ *CHEESE SAUCE*

**Free of:**
Corn
Egg
Soy
Wheat
Yeast

¼ cup green onion, sliced
2 tablespoons butter
2 tablespoons GROUND
   OAT FLOUR (pages 60, 61)

1 cup milk
1 cup (4 ounces)
   shredded Romano cheese

Sauté green onion in butter. Blend in oat flour. Gradually add milk; continue cooking over medium heat, stirring constantly until thickened. Add cheese; stir until cheese is melted. Serve over vegetables, rice dishes, fish, or meat loaf.

**Variations:**

Substitute ¼ cup chopped onion for green onion.
Add ¼ teaspoon oregano or basil leaves.
Add 2 tablespoons grated Parmesan cheese. (This variation is not yeast-free.)

*Makes 1½ cups sauce.*

## □ CREAM SAUCE

| | | |
|---|---|---|
| 2 packages (10 ounces each) frozen cauliflower | salt to taste | **Free of:** |
| | pepper to taste | Corn |
| ½-1 cup pure chicken broth, heated | 1 tablespoon sunflower- seed oil | Egg |
| | | Milk |
| | | Soy |

Cook cauliflower according to package directions until *very* soft. Pour off the cooking water and put cauliflower into blender while still hot. Blend at high speed, slowly adding broth until thick and creamy. Add salt, pepper, and oil. Use immediately, serving over cooked vegetables or meats.

Wheat
Yeast

*Makes approximately 2 cups sauce.*

## □ WHITE SAUCE (CREAM SAUCE)

| | | |
|---|---|---|
| | | **Free of:** |
| 2 tablespoons butter | dash pepper | Corn |
| 2 tablespoons pure wheat pastry flour | dash paprika | Egg |
| | 1 cup milk | Soy |
| ½ teaspoon salt | | Yeast |

About 15 minutes before serving:

In medium-size saucepan, over low heat, melt butter, stir in flour, salt, pepper, and paprika until smooth. Gradually stir in milk; cook, stirring constantly until thickened and smooth.

*Makes 1 cup.*

## Variations:

**Thin white sauce:** Prepare as above, but use 1 tablespoon butter and ¼ cup flour.

**Béchamel sauce:** Prepare as in original recipe for WHITE SAUCE above, but substitute ½ cup chicken broth for half the milk.

**Cheese sauce:** Prepare WHITE SAUCE as above, but halve ingredients and, into hot sauce, stir ½ cup shredded American cheese or Cheddar cheese and ⅛ teaspoon dry mustard; or use 2½ ounces sharp pasteurized processed cheese spread. Cook over low heat, stirring just until cheese is melted. (This recipe is not yeast-free.) *Makes about 1¼ cups.*

**Curry sauce:** When preparing white sauce, to butter add ¼ cup minced onion, 2 teaspoons curry powder, ¾ teaspoon sugar, and ⅛ teaspoon ginger. Just before serving, stir in 1 teaspoon lemon juice. *Makes about 1½ cups.*

## ☐ GRAVY, ALL-PURPOSE

**Free of:**
Corn
Egg
Milk
Soy
Wheat
Yeast

1 tablespoon meat drippings
   or safflower oil
3 RyKrisps, crushed
   to ¼ cup

¼ teaspoon salt*
dash pepper
1 cup pure meat
   stock

*Omit when using seasoned RyKrisp.

Melt drippings in frying pan (or coat pan with oil). Blend in crumbs, salt, and pepper. Add stock gradually. Blend well after each addition. Heat to boiling. Stir constantly. Serve with meat or over potatoes.

*Makes 1 cup.*

# Recipes for Soups

## □ *CHICKEN CHOWDER*

| | | |
|---|---|---|
| 2 cups carrot slices | 1 teaspoon salt | **Free of:** |
| 2 cups water | ½ cup *GROUND OAT* | Corn |
| 1½ cups chopped cooked | *FLOUR (pages 60, 61)* | Egg |
| chicken | 2 cups milk | Soy |
| 2 cups pure chicken | 1½ cups (6 ounces) | Wheat |
| stock | Romano cheese, | Yeast |
| 1 package (10-ounce) frozen | cubed | |
| broccoli, chopped | *CRISPY HERB TOPPING* | |
| ½ cup chopped onion | *(page 154)* | |

Combine carrot, water, chicken stock, broccoli, onion, and salt in 4-quart saucepan or Dutch oven. Bring to a boil over medium-high heat; reduce heat. Cover; simmer about 10 minutes. Bring to a full, rolling boil; gradually add oat flour, stirring constantly. Stir in milk. Simmer, stirring occasionally, about 10 minutes. Remove from heat; stir in cheese. Cover; let stand 3 to 5 minutes before serving. Sprinkle with CRISPY HERB TOPPING to serve.

*Variation:* Substitute 1 10-ounce package frozen chopped spinach for broccoli; omit salt.
*Note:* Additional milk may be added if soup becomes too thick upon standing.

*Makes about 4 1½-cup servings.*

## ☐ *CORN CHOWDER*

**Free of:**
Egg
Soy
Wheat
Yeast

1 cup celery, sliced
3 tablespoons safflower
   oil
¼ cup GROUND OAT FLOUR
   (pages 60, 61)
2 cups milk
1 pound corned beef,
   cut in 1-inch cubes

1 package (10-ounce) frozen
   whole-kernel corn
1 teaspoon dry mustard
   powder
1 cup (4 ounces) shredded
   Romano cheese

Sauté celery in oil in medium-size saucepan. Blend in oat flour. Gradually add milk; continue cooking over medium heat, stirring constantly, until thickened. Reduce heat; add meat, corn, and mustard. Continue cooking over low heat about 5 minutes. Remove from heat; add cheese, mixing until well blended.

*Makes about 4 1-cup servings.*

## □ CORN AND CLAM CHOWDER

| | | |
|---|---|---|
| 1 cup chopped onion | 2 cups diced potatoes | **Free of:** |
| 3 tablespoons safflower oil | ¾ teaspoon salt | Eggs |
| 2 tablespoons potato | ½ teaspoon thyme leaves, | Milk |
| starch | crumbled | Soy |
| 2 cans (10½ ounces each) | 8–10 drops hot-pepper | Wheat |
| whole baby clams | sauce | Yeast |
| water | 2 cups corn kernels, | |
| 1 can (16-ounce) stewed | frozen or canned | |
| tomatoes, cut in pieces | parsley for garnish | |

In a large saucepan, sauté onion in oil for 5 minutes. Stir in potato starch and cook 2 minutes. Drain clams and save juice; add juice to water to make 4 cups; reserve clams.

Stir liquid into saucepan with tomatoes, potatoes, salt, thyme, and hot-pepper sauce; blend well. Bring to boiling point. Cover; reduce heat and simmer 15 minutes. Add corn to saucepan along with reserved clams. Cook 7 minutes longer. Serve garnished with parsley, if desired.

*Makes about 2 quarts.*

## □ CREAMED CELERY SOUP

| | | |
|---|---|---|
| | | **Free of:** |
| ¼ pound butter | 1 cup cream | Corn |
| 1 large onion, finely | 1 cup cold water and | Egg |
| chopped | 2 tablespoons | Soy |
| 1 cup celery, sliced | potato starch, mixed | Wheat |
| 6 cups hot chicken | until smooth | Yeast |
| stock | salt and pepper to season | |
| 2 cups hot milk | | |

Sauté onion and celery in butter until soft. Add chicken stock, hot milk, and cream. Thicken with mixture of water and potato starch. Simmer until thickened and smooth. Whip, if necessary, with wire whisk. Season with salt and pepper to taste.

**Variation:** For casseroles, eliminate the water. This mixture will be similar to canned, condensed cream-of-celery soup.

*Makes about 2 quarts soup.*

## ☐ FISH CHOWDER

**Free of:**
Corn
Egg
Soy
Wheat
Yeast

4 large potatoes, peeled and sliced
3 medium onions, sliced
1 cup chopped celery
1 garlic clove, minced
4 whole cloves
1 tablespoon salt
1 bay leaf
¼ teaspoon dill seed

¼ teaspoon white pepper
2 cups light cream or milk
2 cups water
¼ cup butter
2 packages (16 ounces each) frozen flounder fillets, thawed, or 2 pounds fresh fish fillets

About 50 minutes before serving, in covered, large saucepan, over medium heat, simmer potatoes, onions, celery, garlic, cloves, salt, bay leaf, dill seed, pepper, and 1 cup water about 25 minutes, until tender.

Cut fish into large chunks. Add fish, 1 cup water, and remaining ingredients to vegetables. Cook about 10 minutes, stirring occasionally, until bubbly hot.

*Makes 13 cups, or 8 servings.*

## □ *CREAMED TOMATO SOUP*

| | | |
|---|---|---|
| 2 cups tomatoes, quartered | 2 teaspoons sugar | **Free of:** |
| ½ tablespoon minced onions | 2 tablespoons butter | Corn |
| 1 teaspoon salt | 2 tablespoons potato starch | Egg |
| ¼ teaspoon pepper | 1 quart milk, scalded | Soy |
| dash cayenne pepper | | Wheat |
| | | Yeast |

In large cooking pot, cook tomatoes, onions, salt, pepper, cayenne pepper, and sugar together over medium-high heat for 15 minutes. Strain tomato mixture into a bowl and set aside.

In the cooking pot, melt the butter; blend in the potato starch and gradually add the milk, stirring constantly. Add tomato mixture to the milk mixture and stir until the soup thickens. Serve immediately.

*Makes about 2 quarts soup.*

## □ *MEAT AND VEGETABLE SOUP*

| | | |
|---|---|---|
| 2 tablespoons salt | 1 large onion, diced | **Free of:** |
| 1-2 pounds lean meat, cut in 1-inch cubes | 1 cup potatoes, diced | Corn |
| 12 cups water | ½ of 10-ounce package frozen green beans, French-cut | Egg |
| 1 cup carrots, cut in coins | 2 tablespoons rice | Milk |
| 1 cup celery, diced, with tops | 1 cup frozen peas | Soy |
| ½ cup small rice noodles or rice pasta | 1 can (6-ounce) tomato paste | Wheat |
| ½ medium green pepper, diced | sprinkles of garlic powder, oregano, pepper, dill | Yeast |

Put all ingredients into a large cooking pot and bring the soup to a boil; boil 10 minutes. Turn down the heat and simmer 2½ hours or until the meat is tender.

Refrigerate overnight. Skim fat from top before using, and then heat to serve.

*Makes 4 quarts soup.*

## □ *MEATBALL CHOWDER*

**Free of:**
Corn
Egg
Milk
Soy
Wheat
Yeast

1 pound ground chuck
1 tablespoon safflower oil
6 cups fresh tomatoes,
    peeled and diced
6 cups pure beef broth
2 teaspoons salt
¼ teaspoon pepper
¼ teaspoon garlic powder

2 cups carrots, thinly
    sliced
1 cup raw potatoes, diced
1 cup celery, chopped fine
1 tablespoon fresh parsley
¼ teaspoon thyme
¼ teaspoon basil
2 cups mashed potatoes

Shape ground chuck into meatballs. In large soup pot, brown meatballs in safflower oil. When thoroughly browned, add all other ingredients *except* mashed potatoes and cook until tender, about 1 hour. Add mashed potatoes just before serving, stirring until smooth. Serve immediately.

*Makes 2 to 3 quarts of soup.*

## □ *MEATLESS VEGETABLE SOUP*

**Free of:**
Corn
Egg
Milk
Soy
Wheat
Yeast

½ cup frozen green beans
½ cup diced carrots
½ cup diced celery
½ cup diced potatoes
1 cup shredded cabbage
½ cup frozen peas
2 tablespoons chopped onion

8 cups water
salt and pepper to taste
1 small can tomato puree
1 tablespoon barley
    or rice or both
any other fresh vegetable
    desired except corn

Combine all ingredients in large soup pot. Bring to a boil; then simmer until vegetables are tender. If canned vegetables are used, add just before serving.

*Makes 2 to 3 quarts soup.*

## □ *POTATO SOUP, FRENCH-STYLE*

| | | |
|---|---|---|
| 4 medium potatoes | 1½ cups milk, scalded | **Free of** |
| 3 or 4 leeks, white part | white pepper | Corn |
|   only | 2 egg yolks | Soy |
| 2 tablespoons butter | ready-to-eat crisp rice | Wheat |
| salt to taste |   cereal | Yeast |

Peel and dice potatoes and put in large saucepan. Chop leeks fine and brown lightly in 2 tablespoons butter. Add to potatoes. Add boiling water to cover and ½ teaspoon salt. Cover, bring to boil, and cook until potatoes are tender. Puree entire mixture in blender. Add milk, and heat. Season to taste and beat in egg yolks. Serve with an additional spoonful of butter and a few pieces of cereal in each bowl.

*Makes 4 servings.*

## □ *POTATO AND ONION SOUP*

| | | |
|---|---|---|
| | | **Free of:** |
| | | Corn |
| | | Egg |
| 3 medium onions | 4 cups water | Milk |
| 1 rib celery, chopped | ½–1 teaspoon salt | Soy |
| 4 medium potatoes | ½ cup cashew nuts, raw | Wheat |
| 1 clove garlic |   or dry-roasted | Yeast |

Peel and dice onions, celery, and potatoes. Crush the clove of garlic. Put vegetables into 3- to 4-quart pan with water and salt to taste. Simmer 25 minutes, add nuts, and cook another 5 minutes. Put into blender until smooth. Reheat if necessary. Garnish with chopped parsley.

*Makes 1 quart soup.*

## □ *SPRINGTIME VEGETABLE SOUP*

**Free of:**
Corn
Egg
Milk
Soy
Wheat
Yeast

1 small bunch scallions
8 carrots, young and tender
8 small new potatoes with
    skins

1 small green pepper
1 small, young turnip
4 cups water
chives for garnish

Wash all vegetables. If possible, leave skins on. Put a little water in the blender, add vegetables, and blend until finely chopped. Put into a 3- to 4-quart cooking pot with a total of 4 cups water. Bring to a boil and cook until vegetables are tender but not mushy. Garnish with chopped chives. Serve hot.

### *Variations:*

**Summer:** Add fresh green peas and beans.
**Autumn:** Add sliced green beans and a large onion in place of scallions.
**Winter:** Use large onion in place of spring onions, add celery, and garnish with chopped parsley and nuts.

*Makes about 1 quart soup.*

# □ *WINTER BARLEY SOUP*

2½ pounds lamb stew meat,
   cut in 1½-inch chunks
2 tablespoons safflower oil
6 cups water, hot
½ cup barley
2 medium onions, sliced
2 tablespoons chopped parsley

¼ teaspoon pepper
1 bay leaf
1½ cups chopped celery
1½ cups sliced carrots
½ medium green pepper, diced
¼ teaspoon thyme leaves

**Free of:**
Corn
Egg
Milk
Soy
Wheat
Yeast

About 2½ hours before serving, brown lamb in oil in Dutch oven over medium-high heat; add 6 cups hot water and next 6 ingredients. Simmer, covered, over medium-low heat about 1½ hours.

Stir in remaining ingredients and cook 30 minutes or until meat is tender. Remove bay leaf.

*Makes about 11 cups, or 8 servings.*

# Recipes for Vegetables

## ☐ ANTS ON A LOG

celery stalks                           raisins
natural peanut butter,
  smooth or chunky

Free of:
Corn
Egg
Milk
Soy
Wheat

Wash celery stalks and cut into 3- to 4-inch pieces. Fill groove to the top with peanut butter. Dot peanut butter with raisins. Perfect snack that children can help to prepare.

**Variation:** Fill groove with cream cheese and dot filling with peanuts. Makes a good snack or hors d'oeuvre. (This preparation is not milk-free.)

## □ *CHINESE VEGETABLES*

**Free of:**
Corn
Egg
Milk
Soy
Wheat
Yeast

1 pound fresh green
  beans, carrots, cauliflower,
  broccoli or brussels sprouts
3 tablespoons safflower oil

½ teaspoon sugar
¼ cup pure chicken
  broth

Wash and thinly slice vegetables. Heat oil in large skillet. Add vegetables and toss until coated with oil. Add sugar and broth. Cover skillet; reduce heat; steam for 8 to 10 minutes, shaking the pan occasionally to stir the vegetables. Serve immediately.

*Makes 4 to 6 servings.*

## □ *CUCUMBER CRISPS*

**Free of:**
Corn
Egg
Milk
Soy
Wheat

1½ cups vinegar (4–6
  percent acid)
2½ cups granulated sugar
½ cup kosher salt

1–2 whole cloves garlic
2 onions, finely chopped
cucumbers, peeled and
  sliced ¼-inch thick

Combine ingredients in large glass or plastic bowl. Use enough cucumbers to take up all the liquid. Mix thoroughly. Store in covered jars in the refrigerator. Stir daily, mixing from the bottom. Keeps indefinitely.

## □ *GOLDEN CASSEROLE*

**Free of:**
Corn
Egg
Soy
Wheat
Yeast

6 medium potatoes
1 pint dairy sour cream
10 ounces sharp Cheddar
  cheese, grated
1 bunch green onions,
  chopped
3 tablespoons milk

1 teaspoon salt
⅛ teaspoon pepper
2 tablespoons melted
  butter
1/3 cup ready-to-eat
  crisp rice cereal

Scrub potatoes and cook with skins in boiling salted water until tender. Remove from water and cool. Peel potatoes and chop in ¼-inch cubes. Add sour cream, cheese, onions, milk, salt, and pepper. Mix thoroughly.

Turn into buttered 9x13-inch pan. Smooth top with spatula. Combine melted butter and rice cereal. Sprinkle over top.

Bake at 300°F for 50 minutes or until piping hot. Cut into squares and serve.

*Makes 8 servings.*

## □ GREEN BEAN CASSEROLE

| | | **Free of:** |
|---|---|---|
| 2 packages (10 ounces each) frozen French-style green beans | 1½ cups CREAMED CELERY SOUP (pages 269–70) | Corn |
| ½ cup chopped onions | 1½ cups ready-to-eat crisp rice cereal | Eggs<br>Soy<br>Wheat<br>Yeast |

Partially cook beans according to package directions. Drain and stir in the onions, half the cereal, and all the soup. (If too thick, add up to ½ cup milk.)

Bake in greased, covered 1½-quart baking dish at 350°F for 15 minutes. Sprinkle remaining cereal over top and bake uncovered 5 minutes more.

*Makes 6 to 8 servings.*

## □ POTATO-VEGETABLE PIE

| | | **Free of:** |
|---|---|---|
| 3 medium potatoes | 1 small zucchini, thinly sliced, with the skin on | Corn |
| milk and butter to taste | | Egg |
| 2 tablespoons sesame seeds, not toasted | 2–3 carrots, shaved | Soy |
| ¼–½ green pepper, diced | 2 medium tomatoes, thinly sliced | Wheat |
| 1 medium onion, chopped fine | ¾–1 cup shredded Romano cheese | Yeast |

Boil the potatoes in their skins until they are fork-tender, but they should not fall apart when tested. Mash them with the skins on, adding milk and butter to taste. Consistency should be soft but not runny. Add sesame seeds and mix well. Press into a buttered 8- or 9-inch pie pan to form the crust of the pie.

In medium-size frying pan, sauté together in a small amount of butter the green pepper and onion. When onion is transparent, add the zucchini, and continue sautéing 1 minute longer, or until zucchini is fork-tender. When almost done, add the shaved carrot and cook 1 more minute. Pour mixture into the potato crust and cover with the tomatoes.

Top with the Romano cheese. Bake at 350°F for 30 minutes or until the cheese is melted and beginning to bubble.

May be used either as side dish or entree.

*Makes 6 servings.*

## □ *SPINACH SOUFFLÉ*

**Free of:**
Corn
Milk
Soy
Wheat
Yeast

*1 package (10-ounces)*
*frozen spinach*
*1 cup pure beef or*
*chicken broth*

*2 eggs, separated*
*2 tablespoons potato*
*starch*

Cook spinach in broth instead of water until tender; follow directions on the package. Put spinach and broth in blender, adding egg yolks and potato starch. Puree mixture.

In small bowl with mixer, beat egg whites until stiff. Fold spinach mixture into egg whites. Bake in greased 1½-quart casserole dish at 350°F for 30 to 45 minutes or until knife comes out clean when inserted into the middle of the soufflé. Serve hot.

*Makes 4 servings.*

## □ *PUFFED SPUDS*

| | | Free of: |
|---|---|---|
| 4 cups mashed potatoes | 2 tablespoons instant | Corn |
| 1 package (8-ounces) | minced onion | Soy |
| cream cheese | 1 egg, beaten | Wheat |
| | | Yeast |

Combine ingredients. Pour into greased 1¾-quart casserole dish. Bake uncovered at 350°F for 45 minutes or until top is golden.

*Makes 8 ½-cup servings.*

## □ *STIR-FRY VEGETABLES*

| | | Free of: |
|---|---|---|
| ¾ cup water | ½ cup French-style | Corn |
| 1 cup pure beef or | green beans | Egg |
| chicken broth | 1 tablespoon potato starch | Milk |
| ½ cup chopped onions | ½ cup cold water | Soy |
| ½ cup chopped celery | salt to taste | Wheat |
| ½ cup bean sprouts | steamed rice for 4 servings | Yeast |
| | crisp rice noodles | |

In 10-inch skillet or large saucepan, bring ¾ cup water to a boil with broth. Add onion and celery; cook over medium heat until tender, about 10 mintues. Add bean sprouts and green beans; cook about 5 minutes until beans are tender.

In small cup, combine potato starch and cold water, mixing until smooth. Add slowly to vegetable mixture, stirring constantly until sauce is thickened and transparent.

Other vegetables that may be combined in this way are:
   zucchini, sliced thin
   cucumber, sliced thin
   carrots, sliced thin
   green peas, fresh or frozen
   tomatoes, cut in wedges

Cooked meat or poultry may also be added if the vegetables are to be used as a main dish. Then serve with steamed rice and crisp rice noodles.

*Makes 3 to 4 servings.*

## □ *ZUCCHINI PARMESAN*

**Free of:**
Corn
Egg
Soy
Wheat
Yeast

1 onion, sliced
¼ cup butter
4 to 6 zucchini, scrubbed
   and cut into ¼-inch
   rounds

¼ teaspoon salt
⅛ teaspoon pepper
½ cup grated Parmesan
   cheese

In large skillet, sauté onion in butter until transparent. Add zucchini, salt, and pepper, and cook, tossing lightly, for about 5 minutes. Add cheese just before serving and toss lightly to coat well.

*Makes 4 servings.*

# MASTER RECIPE INDEX

# INDEX:
# The
# Allergy
# Cookbook
# &
# Food-Buying
# Guide